Adopting Open Source Software

Adopting Open Source Software
A Practical Guide

Brian Fitzgerald, Jay P. Kesan, Barbara Russo,
Maha Shaikh, and Giancarlo Succi

The MIT Press
Cambridge, Massachusetts
London, England

For information about special quantity discounts, please email special_sales@mitpress.mit.edu

This book was set in Sabon by Graphic Composition, Inc. Printed and bound in the United States of America.

Library of Congress Cataloging-in-Publication Data

Adopting open source software : a practical guide / Brian Fitzgerald . . . [et al.].
    p. cm.
Includes bibliographical references and index.
ISBN 978-0-262-51635-8 (pbk. : alk. paper)
1. Software configuration management—Case studies. 2. Open source software—Case studies. 3. Support services (Management)—Data processing—Case studies. I. Fitzgerald, Brian, 1959 Oct. 12–.
QA76.76.C69A35 2011
005.3—dc22
                                            2011003571

10 9 8 7 6 5 4 3 2 1

Contents

Introduction

Governments and public institutions have embraced the fruits of technology in a reluctant and uncomfortable manner. This is not altogether surprising, given that technology is an area that is often outside of the core competency of many policy makers. Such reluctance and lack of expertise are untenable among policy makers, however, because technology, and information technology in particular, is an important part of daily life and increasingly is the medium through which citizens interact with government. This book attempts to empower policy makers with the knowledge and judgment to make decisions related to the deployment of information technology, particularly open source software (OSS), in public institutions. The ultimate goal is to ensure that citizens are empowered to deal with governments in an effective and cost-efficient manner, with reliable and complete information and with enhanced confidence in government processes.

The openness of code and the OSS development process help to encourage the transparency regarding how the system works that is crucial for helping to empower citizens. OSS was developed as a method of software distribution and testing and has become a method of software production that is accompanied by flexible licensing and a potential means of invention and social aggregation that is characterized by growth and open diffusion. OSS was initially dismissed by media and academics as nothing more than a fad, but the open source phenomenon has grown, mutated, and rapidly been adopted by private and public organizations to the extent that it is difficult to find any area of software development in which OSS is not in use (Fitzgerald 2006). One intriguing facet of the open source phenomenon is the effect it has had on fields and methods of organizing information outside of software development—for example, crowdsourcing of ideas, the move toward open collaboration as a better form of innovation, open government, and open standards. The degree of diffusion of OSS can be perceived, for example, in flourishing public Web-based code repositories, such as SourceForge and Apache, which were created to control and manage software and provide information, articles, news, references, and forums to help those who use or are about to use OSS.

The widespread diffusion of OSS has been driven by five socioeconomic factors: (1) the establishment of large OSS communities of individuals who fulfill specific user requests, (2) potential reductions in the costs of licenses and the constraints posed by commercial software products, (3) the support of companies such as Sun and IBM that have adopted OSS as a new business model they use to compete against firms that sell proprietary software products or defend their hardware products, (4) the expansion and dissemination of OSS through extensive creative licensing, and (5) the perceived interest of public institutions that have limited budget and resources and that make use of OSS to maintain and update their information technology (IT) infrastructure. Favorable circumstances and a favorable environment, including new instruments of social communication over the Internet—chat, forum, and social networks—and fast connections, have done the rest. OSS is distributed through the Web and has become a reality in the IT market, and users who initially perceived OSS as a novelty perceive it as a new opportunity.

Does all of this potential qualify OSS as an innovative technology? Is OSS a new viable alternative for individuals, firms, and public organizations? There is an ongoing debate about this issue (Fuggetta 2003). The major point of discussion is whether OSS is an innovation, because it is not an invention that originated with identifiable new ideas. In other words, OSS products are not inventions solely because they are open source. In fact, being open source is not a new idea. In its earliest manifestations, software was open, although not as a commercial good. Furthermore, being open source does not mean that the software has been generated as a result of new ideas. The majority of the OSS products were developed from ideas similar to the existing products of their proprietary counterparts. In terms of their overall functionality, Linux and Apache offer an alternative to existing proprietary software. In addition, the collaborative and distributed approach of OSS development dates back to the 1960s (Feller and Fitzgerald 2002) and was already evident in the early 1980s. At that time, collaborative ferment permeated research centers and inspired people such as Richard Stallman, the founder of the free software philosophy, which is an integral part of OSS, during his time at the Massachusetts Institute of Technology and Barry Boehm, the creator of the win–win spiral development, a collaborative method that has been adopted by many software firms.

However, whether OSS is an innovation depends to a large degree on how one defines and understands the concept of an innovation. The work of van de Ven, Polley, Garud, and Venkataraman (2008) distinguishes an invention from an innovation. An invention is a new idea, and an innovation is a broader concept that includes both the development and implementation of a new idea. This work stresses that an innovation need not be new to everybody and might even be seen as a copy, but it must be novel to at least some stakeholders. Van de Ven and colleagues' definition encompasses both product and process ideas concerning novelty (technical artifact and practice-related/procedural issues). That definition is similar to the widely accepted definition of Trott (1998). Trott identified innovation as the combination of theoretical concept, technical invention, and commercial exploitation, in which ideas are transformed into inventions, and innovation is the overall process that transforms ideas into market objects (Myers and Marquis 1969). The primary distinction between these definitions is the commercial exploitation element. According to Trott, "The process to convert intellectual thoughts into a tangible new artefact . . . is invention. This is where science and technology play a significant role . . . Innovation depends on inventions but inventions need to be harnessed by commercial activities before they can contribute to the growth of an organization" (Trott 1998). Trott defines *new* as what is perceived to be new by individuals and not what is determined by the elapsed time of discovery (Rogers 1962; Rogers and Shoemaker 1972). Neither invention nor innovation need to be determined by ideas that are new in terms of time. Given these premises, OSS is innovation. The main merit of OSS is that it is a catalyst for skills and good practices relating to quality software development and provides a novel mechanism for competition among IT providers. The five case studies presented in chapters 3 through 7 show that the actors and organizations took into account how a novel tool or application would be incorporated into organizational practices.

If innovation is the process of introducing objects to the market, then adoption is the process of introducing an object from the market into organizations. As is true for innovation, technology adoption is a complex process that is affected by social, economic, and technical factors, and OSS is no exception. In addition, complexity can be amplified with OSS, because OSS has not traditionally supplied information on its technical or business standards. OSS communities typically focus on specific technical support for installing and configuring their tools, but they do not seek to provide standards, documentation, manuals, and case studies that can help users and managers involved in the adoption of the technology.

Gallivan (2001) proposed a framework for the adoption of technological innovations within organizations. His framework acknowledges that, within organizations, authoritarian decisions of technology adoption are more common than allowing users to choose adoption. This derives from Weberian (Weber 1948) ideas of bureaucracy to which most public organizations (and most private companies that grow beyond a certain manageable size) adhere.

Relatively few works have tackled the acceptance and adoption of OSS to date (e.g., Gallego, Luna, and Bueno 2008; Ozel et al. 2007) or have explored OSS diffusion within specific organizations, such as public administrations (e.g., Ozel et al. 2007; Fitzgerald and Kenny 2003; Rossi et al. 2006b; Russo,

Braghin et al. 2005; Ven, Van Nuffel, and Verelst 2006). The limited amount of research highlights one important fact: OSS is a strategic challenge that enables public organizations to modernize within limited budgets and with limited resources (Russo, Succi, and Zuliani 2003; Rossi et al. 2006a). There is a related concern regarding long-term costs of OSS—that costs are being transferred from proprietary software products to software services, which become increasingly expensive over the long run.

The implementation of strategies of innovation is not straightforward, and OSS is no exception. The discrepancy between a strategic decision and its strategic implementation— which is known as the *assimilation gap*—can be substantial. For example, one factor that is known to cause this gap in OSS is the negative attitude of potential adopters regarding such a technology, particularly if the adoption is mandated by management. Potential adopters might believe that mandating the use of the cheaper open source technology lowers the value of their work because "management does not invest in their work." This negative attitude creates resistance and can even determine whether the adoption project fails (Fitzgerald 2009).

This book presents a framework for OSS adoption based on Gallivan's (2001) work and applies it to five public organizations (see chapter 2 for an explanation of Gallivan's framework). This framework can be used to determine which factors enable or inhibit the implementation of strategies for OSS adoption within public organizations. Actual experiences involving mass OSS adoption and diffusion are presented in chapters 3 through 7. The traditional theory of technology diffusion specifies that mass adoption is known as *secondary adoption* when it becomes the concrete implementation of the strategic decision to engage in adoption, which is known as *primary adoption.* Secondary adoption is a complex process that Gallivan (2001) conceptualizes as involving both individual and organizational aspects. Secondary adoption also requires lengthy, extensive investigation because it relates to the prolonged process of absorption and acceptance of a technology by a variety of users. The assimilation gap measures the misalignment between primary and secondary adoption (Fichman and Kemerer 1997, 1999). This book focuses on analyzing OSS as a diffusion phenomenon in terms of secondary adoption in public organizations. However, before moving onto the framework and case studies, it is important to outline the basic features that distinguish public administration organizations from private companies. This will contextualize the case studies and highlight the need for and relevance of this book.

FACETS AND FEATURES OF PUBLIC ADMINISTRATION

The case studies in chapters 3 through 7 show that examples of OSS adoption by public administrations share some common features. Governments link the idea of open source to pertinent issues of democracy through openness, public accountability through greater transparency, greater competition through increased vendor choice, reduction of vendor lock-in, increased access to citizens and vice versa through open and easier methods of communication and collaboration, online supply of services to citizens, and greater efficiency of public services through delivery involving open source and open standards.

There is a belief that the more open a government is, the better the democratic processes work. Indeed, governments often appear more democratic if they provide interactive forums for discussion between the elected and the governed. Ideas regarding open source have expanded to include such forums but should be treated cautiously by both public employees and citizens. Citizens need to understand whether promises made in discussion with public employees are valid and believable. Is the citizen's information safe and secure when shared in such forums? Public employees must consider the words they use carefully when they are in online contact with citizens. The greater the volume of communication between public employees and citizens, the greater the possibility of conflict, misunderstanding, and the possibility of promises being made that may not be kept.

On the other hand, there is the very real potential that more democratic procedures and vibrant market competition will emerge when open source ideas, interoperable software, and standards are adopted. Greater collaboration and transparency can lead to more trust between governments and their citizens. There is a possibility that long-term relationships can be built and that governments can find out more about what the citizens really want and need in their communities. It is also a good tool for campaigning and outreach.

The related issue of public accountability has been well researched in the fields of e-government and new public management. This book will touch on it lightly simply to show how transparency in the legal system, openness of documents, and access of citizens to increased amounts of information can lead to a sense of better public accountability.

The manner in which this is implemented in practice varies, and access to information is a complicated issue that raises concerns regarding how much information is enough, the need for security versus privacy, who holds this information and how it is held, how quickly it is updated, whether there is unfettered access to information across different software applications, and so forth. All of these concerns can be manipulated in favor of governments that want to hold on to information should they be so inclined. These are real concerns that can become problematic when openness is encouraged in public organizations.

Openness and transparency are linked to accountability and, in a more general sense (moving beyond public organizations), are regarded as key elements of open source and other forms of innovation. The question then arises: what are the driving factors behind incentivizing innovation in public organizations?

INNOVATION IN PUBLIC ORGANIZATIONS

Is innovation as important in public organizations as it is in private ones? Some people would argue that it depends on what sorts of services are being offered by the public organization. If there is a need for stability in the organization, then innovation might produce more problems than advantages. If there is agreement that innovation is a good thing, then it is both important and relevant to assess how, when, why, and in what way public organizations can be encouraged to innovate.

It has been argued that public organizations lack a culture of innovation because change is not seen in a good light by employees or by citizens who need to develop liaisons with public organizations. There is even less incentive to innovate because promotion ladders are not linked to innovation, unlike in private organizations. Private organizations work on the basis of profit and often anticipate that new ideas might lead to increased revenues and profits. Public organizations need to deliver services, and the degree of efficiency with which this is done is usually not open to question. There are also differences in the mindsets of public employees in comparison with private sector employees. In many countries, public jobs are jobs for life, which usually means that complacency can creep in and dampen the desire for change. Finally, innovations have implications for change in legal structures, standards, and so forth, which are not straightforward or easy to achieve in short order. The question of how to encourage innovation in public organizations thus does not have a straightforward answer.

PUBLIC VERSUS PRIVATE ORGANIZATIONS

The central aim for public organizations is service delivery, while for the private sector it is competition and profit. Thus, the use, motivation for adoption, implementation styles, and encouragement of innovation practices differ for these sectors. A great deal of literature has focused on the private sector's adoption of OSS. However, the growing importance of the need of openness in government indicates that this subject merits scrutiny. On the one hand, the commercial application of OSS helps perpetuate the use and adoption of OSS beyond small hacker circles. On the other hand, the adoption of open source by public organizations promises to keep the original ideology of OSS and its development style alive.

OSS adoption by commercial organizations centers on emerging business models and how to adapt these models to allow for profit-making with a product that requires one to release the secret sauce of the product along with the product. Even so, there is significant competition among various suppliers of open source products, such as Red Hat Linux, Fedora, and CentOS. Exclusionary patterns of competition are emerging among them. Public organizations, as the case studies described in chapters 3 through 7 show, are at the other end of the spectrum, where giving away the source code and adoption by other public administrations are encouraged and imperative.

The commercial application and adoption of OSS has hybridized how open source is developed, shifted licenses (many new licenses are introduced every few months), tilted the balance in favor of company-employed hackers in communities instead of volunteers, and evolved practices of communication and governance that are more in keeping with the sort of control found in private companies. Some academics (Asay 2006; Roberts, Hann, and Slaughter 2006) debate the idea that there may soon be a day when open source as we know it will no longer survive the rigors of commercial adoption. On the other hand, when public organizations adopt OSS, they tend to do so in a manner that is close to the original open source ideology, which stresses openness, transparency, communication, and collaboration. These motives are the source of many of the slogans of open government initiatives around the world today.

OPENNESS AND INCREASED PARTICIPATION IN PUBLIC ADMINISTRATION: LESSONS AND RISKS

Openness is an idea that goes beyond software (be it OSS or proprietary) and encourages a more participatory form of communication. The case studies in this book reveal some interesting qualities that can help governments reach out to the citizenry. The cases show that adopting OSS or openness on any level is not easy. There are financial issues involved when implementing a new system, regardless of whether a license is involved. While the total cost of ownership diminishes over time for OSS, the short-term costs of moving away from legacy systems are substantial and are similar for both OSS and proprietary software projects.

OSS raises new and novel legal issues. While it is true that OSS involves open licensing, legal systems (which are notoriously slow to change and adapt in most countries) need to keep abreast of the amendments that are necessary for coping with OSS. This impacts public administration procedures. It can slow down the acceptance of new products and practices and make it difficult to innovate in either area. Major barriers are cultural differences and acceptance (this is made clear in the comparative analysis in chapter 8). The implications of such risks are often harder to assess in public administrations due to the complex nature of the interactions between such organizations and with the private sector. This complexity is linked to the insular nature of decision making in public organizations. Citizens may find this caution annoying, but it often stems from legitimate reasons: privacy concerns, legal systems, and cumbersome decision-making procedures.

Increased participation within a public organization, let alone with citizens, necessarily entails a need for time and patience before anything can be accomplished. Collaboration is important but brings with it coordination issues and a need for privacy (at some level) balanced with transparency. Who should be included in decision making? It is impossible to take into account every possible opinion. How are opinions judged, how are views collected, and how is structure brought to bear on the many points of view? Public employees are often evaluated on single-author contributions to reports, so how can they be encouraged to contribute to forums and group discussions? Does this entail a new system of evaluation, and, if so, how quickly and efficiently can it be rolled out across all public organizations? How standardized are such evaluation systems in the sense that public employees will feel that they are being measured using sound standards and that they are able to move across public organizations should they choose to do so? Do citizens or public employees feel left out if their ideas are not incorporated? These and other issues plague public administrations that attempt to move toward greater openness and participation through OSS and open standards.

GOALS OF THIS BOOK

The primary goal of this book is to trace the adoption of OSS in different public organizations and to present how and why people adopted OSS and what consequences followed. In particular, the book discusses which factors can affect the decision to adopt OSS and who benefits from OSS adoption.

The second goal of this book is to collect the contemporary best practices and lessons for specifying, evolving (i.e., when to use open source and how such adoption should adapt and increase over time), and governing OSS secondary adoptions using sound and proven case studies (see table 8.1). The third goal of this book is to feed an insatiable curiosity about successful OSS adoptions, investigating questions such as: "How did they do that?" and "What was distinctive about their adoption practices, process, or motivation?" Exposing the story of adoption by studying its facilitators and inhibitors on the individual and organizational levels can help offer inspiration to managers and practitioners who want to build upon the experiences of well-defined OSS adoption processes.

This book uses a strong, theoretically grounded framework for analyzing five significant real-world cases of OSS adoption. It is first of its kind; conventional wisdom has yet to emerge in this area, and, thus, no other material exists that can help guide practices in this area. In addition, the mix of a theoretical framework and real-world applications allows the global research community to build on this work while also providing practitioners with advice and information about best practices.

The framework defined in chapter 2 serves as a useful structuring framework that allows the stories of OSS adoption in chapters 3 through 7 to be told in a similar way, although each case study draws on different aspects of the framework (as might be expected). Chapter 8 draws out these differences and points out the major motivations that have driven organizations to implement and adopt OSS.

This book is written for managers, public officials, and scholars who seek inspiration from sound and proven OSS secondary adoption experiences beyond their current domain of expertise and who want to learn about contemporary best practices for specifying, evolving, and managing OSS in public organizations.

ORGANIZATION OF THIS BOOK

This book is organized into eight chapters. Chapter 1 introduces basic terminology needed to follow the remaining chapters, including standard definitions of terms regarding the open source domain and technology adoption. In addition, the chapter contains a brief introduction to the history of open source and its evolution. This chapter cites major references that can be consulted for additional information and briefly summarizes OSS products considered in the following chapters. Chapter 2 introduces the framework for OSS adoption. Chapters 3 through 7 present five case studies, and chapter 8 is dedicated to a comparative analysis of these studies with different domains, contexts, and OSS products. It identifies and illustrates differences in motivation, strategies, technologies, and socioeconomic aspects.

1
Background and Definitions

This section introduces common terminology concerning the adoption of technologies and OSS. Expert readers can skip this part of the book or refer to the table of terms at the end of this chapter.

• *Open source software (OSS), free software, and libre software*   OSS is software whose source code has been published and is made available to the public. Anyone can copy, modify, and redistribute the source code without paying royalties or fees but must respect and quote the original contributions. Open source code is developed and maintained by open source communities. These communities are virtual communities of practitioners who use the Internet to share project artifacts (Rogers 2003). Individual programmers/users and companies participate in these communities and their projects. Access is open to everyone. Examples of open source projects include Linux, Eclipse, Apache, Mozilla, OpenOffice.org (OpenOffice), and various projects hosted in online repositories such as SourceForge, Ohloh, and Slashdot.

The term *open source* is widely used but also relatively new. It was coined by a group of proponents (including Eric S.

Raymond and Tim O'Reilly) in February 1998 as a marketing device to overcome what they saw as the antibusiness bias
of the free software movement established in 1985 by Richard Stallman (Feller and Fitzgerald 2002; Di Bona, Ockman,
and Stone 1999). They established the Open Source Initiative
to promote the open source definition (OSD) (<http://open
source.org/docs/osd>) and certify software licenses that were
OSD compliant.

The term *open source* has evolved since its initial definition.
The metamorphosis is described in an article by Fitzgerald
(2006):

> The open source software phenomenon has metamorphosed into a
> more mainstream and commercially viable form, which I label as
> OSS 2.0 . . . The development process becomes less bazaar-like as
> strategic planning becomes paramount. Analysis and design are
> more deliberate as the model spreads to vertical product domains.
> Developers are increasingly being paid to work on open source.
> More sophisticated business models are emerging and employed in
> a hybrid fashion. Customers are willing to pay the going rate for the
> whole product in terms of support, which in turn can be delivered
> by a bazaar network of interested parties that provide varied but
> complementary services. Licensing also moves to the fore as propri-
> etary companies produce licenses that comply with the open source
> definition, while open source companies seek to raise money through
> licensing. Given this complex melting pot, a number of significant
> implications and challenges for research and practice emerge.

Stallman initially championed the Open Source Initiative but
later dissociated himself from it while continuing to promote
the term *free software*. The original definition used the term
free to describe software that is open and accessible to anyone,
which harmonizes with the principles of the Free Software
Foundation of Stallman (<http://www.fsf.org>). Stallman argues that there are basic ethical and philosophical differences

between free software and OSS (Stallman 2002). *Free—*according to Stallman—does not refer to cost but rather to freedom of software users to modify source code for their own purposes and the freedom to redistribute the modified software freely. The term *libre* has the same meaning as the English word *free* but stresses the freedom to modify and distribute such software in non-English-speaking countries.

Free software and libre software are contemporary terms associated with OSS. In this spirit, the new term *FLOSS* (free/frei, libre, open source software) seeks to aggregate these concepts. This book acknowledges the differences among these concepts but will treat these terms as synonyms.

• *Proprietary software* Proprietary software is distributed under commercial license agreements, usually for a fee. The primary difference between commercial software licenses and OSS licenses is that the recipient does not normally receive any right to copy, modify, or redistribute commercial software without paying fees or royalties.

• *Standards* In technical usage, a standard is an example of an item or a specification against which others can be measured and are produced by many organizations. Some standards are for internal usage only, while other standards are for use by groups of people, groups of companies, or a subsection of an industry. Problems can arise when groups come together and have incompatible standards.

There are many national standards. The International Organization for Standardization (ISO) is based in Geneva, Switzerland, and has established tens of thousands of standards covering almost every conceivable topic. Most of these ISO standards have been adopted worldwide and have replaced incompatible home-grown standards. Many of the ISO's standards evolved naturally from standards designed in-house within an industry or by a particular country, while other standards were developed from scratch by groups of experts who sit on various technical committees. According to the ISO (<http://www.iso.org>), data standards are:

... documented agreements containing technical specifications or other precise criteria to be used consistently as rules, guidelines, or definitions of characteristics, to ensure that materials, products, processes and services are fit for their purpose.

Standards can be de facto, meaning they are followed for the sake of convenience, or de jure, meaning they are used as a result of (more or less) legally binding contracts and documents. Government agencies often must follow standards issued by official standardization organizations.

The term *data standard* refers to the class of standards used in information processing in its broadest sense. For example, there are standards for moving information over computer networks (e.g., TCP/IP, HTTP, FTP), and there are standards for displaying characters of different languages (e.g., UNICODE). Work on standards typically focuses on protocols for interoperability and communication (e.g., XML, HTTP) and text documents (e.g., .rtf, .doc). This book focuses on data standards for storing information and considers text documents as well as spreadsheets, images, and drawings.

• *Proprietary data standards* Proprietary data standards have been developed by and controlled by a given company and have not been made freely available for adoption by the industry.

• *Open data standards* Open data standards (ODS) are formats that are openly documented, have been accepted through either formal or de facto processes, and are freely available for adoption. The formal definition of ODS varies according to the context of implementation. The European Commission issued the following definition (<http://ec.europa.eu/idabc>) of ODS for public organizations within e-government's interoperability framework:

• The standard is adopted and will be maintained by a not-for-profit organization, and its ongoing development occurs on the basis of an open decision-making procedure that is available to all interested parties (e.g., consensus or majority decision).

• The standard has been published, and the standard specification document is available either for free or at a nominal charge. It must be permissible for all parties to copy, distribute, and use it for no fee or for a nominal fee.

• The intellectual property—that is, patents—of (parts of) the standard is irrevocably made available on a royalty-free basis.

• There are no constraints on the reuse of the standard.

Examples of ODS include HTTP, HTML, TEX, RDF, CSV, WAP, TCP/IP, XML, and SQL. They are typically developed by software engineers from various IT/software companies who collaborate under the auspices of organizations such as the World Wide Web Consortium (W3C), the Organization for the Advancement of Structured Information Standards (OASIS), the Open Mobile Alliance (OMA), and the Internet Engineering Task Force (IETF).

• *Innovation* "An innovation is an idea, practice, or object that is perceived as new by an individual or other unit of adoption. It matters little, so far as human behavior is concerned, whether or not an idea is 'objectively' new as measured by the lapse of time since its first use or discovery . . . New in an innovation need not just involve new knowledge" (Rogers 2003). Often *innovation* is used as a synonym for *technology*, as in technology adoption and innovation adoption. As a matter of fact, however, the two terms are different (Rogers 2003) (see also *technology*). This book distinguishes between technology adoption and innovation diffusion in order to make this difference clear.

This work considers open source to be a phenomenon of innovation. It would be inappropriate and generally untrue to refer to OSS simply as new technology. In order to better understand the definition of innovation, the reader should consider the OpenOffice suite, which is not simply a new technology for personal productivity, as was the case for 99% of the features of Microsoft Office, but is also innovative in a way that makes it accessible.

• *Diffusion of innovation*   "Diffusion is the process in which innovation is communicated through certain channels over time among the members of a social system. It is special type of communication, in that the messages are concerned with new ideas" (Rogers 1962). This is the concept that underlies methods, instruments, facts, and artifacts that are discussed in this book: innovation as new ideas and diffusion as a special type of communication. This is the meaning to emphasize with the OSS phenomenon; it concerns a new idea that is relevant to software development, distribution, and use that utilizes innovative channels and methods of two-way communication.

The theory of diffusion of innovation focuses on factors that facilitate or inhibit adoption within organizations. The process of diffusion has two major stages: *primary adoption*, in which the decision is made at the strategic level that comprises evaluation and selection, and *secondary adoption*, which refers to the actual adoption and use by individuals throughout the organization (Gallivan 2001). Primary and secondary adoption often do not exist in perfect symbiosis (Bradford and Florin 2003). For example, effective secondary adoption can be impacted by social and technical factors that can slow or stop the innovation process that was defined on the strategic level during the primary adoption phase (Cooper and Zmud 1990). The gap between the strategic decision and the actual use of innovation is known as the assimilation gap (Fichman and Kemerer 1999). The model proposed by Rogers (Rogers 2003) is based on more than 3,000 case studies and is founded on factors that include technology innovation, personal and organizational characteristics, and the surrounding environment. The degree of diffusion of innovation is measured in terms of the rate of adoption and the achievement of the critical mass (Rogers 2003; Markus 1987). Diffusion of innovation involves three types of decision-making processes: optional decisions, collective decisions, and authority decisions with respect to the decrease in individual responsibility for the decision. This distinction was clear at the time of the Rogers' model, but traditional research has focused on individual adopters and optional decisions. During the 1990s, Fichman (1992) proposed a form of implementation of Rogers' traditional framework that stressed the relevance of managerial intervention, interdependencies between adopters, and organizational characteristics.

• *Technology* Technology is a design for instrumental action that reduces the type of uncertainty in the cause–effect relationship that involves achieving the desired outcome (Rogers 2003). A technology is typically determined by its hard and soft parts. IT stresses the soft part of a technology and focuses on the support provided by operations, management, and decision making.

• *Technology adoption*   Technology adoption is the process of adopting a technology in a given organization or a group. The theory of technology adoption is founded on several types of research, including the diffusion of innovation (Rogers 1962), the theory of reasoned actions (Fishbein and Ajzen 1975), the technology acceptance model (Davis 1989), the theory of planned behaviors (Ajzen 1985; Taylor and Todd 1995), and social cognitive theory (Compeau and Higgins 1995). Each of these theories contributes a different perspective to the foundations of technology adoption, although some of these theories stem from disciplines other than information systems, such as social sciences. The theory of reasoned actions centers on behavioral intentions—in the context of this book, behavioral intentions regarding the adoption of a technology. The theory has been revised and extended by Ajzen into the theory of planned behavior. The technology acceptance model is used to measure the acceptance of a technology using two major factors: perceived usefulness and perceived ease of use. Social cognitive theory originated with social issues research concerning learning methods that are based on imitative behavior. This theory states that the adoption of a technology can be facilitated by observing the behavior of others. One type of technology adoption is IT adoption, which stresses the soft concept of technology (Rogers 2003).

• *Transformational government*   The concept of transformational government was introduced by the British government in 2007 (Chief Information Officer Council, UK Government

2007) as a form of evolution of e-government, in which the major goal is enabling electronic services. Transformational government instead seeks to get the best out of the available technologies. As such, transformational government focuses on how technology improves the operations of public bodies with respect to the needs of citizens, front- and back-office optimization, and managerial professionalism. This perspective views open technologies as an opportunity for the professional growth of public officers and managers.

Table 1.1 summarizes the key terms defined in this chapter.

Table 1.1
Technology Adoption and Open Source Software Terms

Term	Description	Major reference(s)
Diffusion of innovation	Diffusion is the process by which innovation is communicated through certain channels over time among the members of a social system. It is a special type of communication in which the messages concern new ideas.	Rogers 1962, 2003
Innovation	An innovation is an idea, practice, or object that is perceived as new by an individual or other unit of adoption. It matters little, so far as human behavior is concerned, whether an idea is objectively new as measured by the lapse of time since its first use or discovery. New is an innovation need and does not just involve only new knowledge.	Rogers 1962, 2003; Trott 1998
Open source software (OSS)	OSS is software whose source code is published and made available to the public so that anyone can copy, modify, and redistribute the source code without paying royalties or fees, while respecting and quoting the original contributions.	Open Source Initiative (<http://www.open source.org/docs/osd>)

Table 1.1
(continued)

Term	Description	Major reference(s)
Free software	Free software is open and accessible to anyone according to the principles of the Free Software Foundation of Stallman.	Free Software Foundation (<http://www.fsf.org>)
Libre software	Libre software stresses the freedom of software in non-English-speaking countries and makes use of the same meaning of free.	GNU Operating System (<http://www.gnu.org>)
Open data standards	Open data standards are openly documented and have been accepted through either formal or de facto processes and are freely available for adoption.	International Organization for Standardization (<http://www.iso.org>), Interoperable Delivery of European eGovernment Services to public Administrations, Businesses and Citizens (<http://ec.europa.eu/idabc>)
Proprietary data standards	Proprietary data standards are developed by and controlled by a given company and have not been made freely available for adoption by the industry.	—
Proprietary software	Proprietary software is distributed under commercial license agreements, usually for a fee.	—

Table 1.1
(continued)

Term	Description	Major reference(s)
Standard	A standard is an example of an item or a specification against which all others may be measured.	International Organization for Standardization (<http://www.iso.org>)
Technology	Technology is a design for instrumental action that reduces the uncertainty in the cause–effect relationship involved in achieving the desired outcome.	Rogers 1962
Technology adoption	Technology adoption is the process of adopting a technology in a given organization. The theory of technology adoption studies the factors that influence adoption.	Davis 1989
Transformational government enabled by technology	Transformational government improves the operations of public bodies with respect to the needs of citizens, front- and back-office optimization, and managerial professionalism.	Chief Information Officer Council, UK Government 2007

2

A Framework for Investigating OSS Adoption

INTRODUCTION

This chapter derives and discusses a framework for investigating the adoption of OSS, with particular emphasis on secondary deployment, meaning the actual adoption of OSS by individuals throughout an organization following the primary organizational decision to adopt an innovation. A large amount of research has been conducted on the adoption of technological innovations, and a number of frameworks for analysis exist for this purpose. This book draws upon a framework derived by Gallivan (2001). This chapter explains the rationale for choosing this framework, including the components behind the framework and a discussion of how they are relevant in an open source context. Subsequent chapters use this framework to discuss five cases of OSS adoption.

A FRAMEWORK FOR STUDYING SECONDARY ADOPTION OF TECHNOLOGICAL INNOVATIONS

Gallivan's (2001) longitudinal research into the deployment of innovative client-server technology reviewed the major traditional frameworks of technology adoption. Rogers' (1962,

2003) classic work in this area has been the basis for a substantial amount of innovation adoption research (e.g., Kwon
and Zmud 1987; Cooper and Zmud 1990; Swanson 1994;
Chau and Tam 1997; Bajaj 2000; Gallivan 2001).

Gallivan concluded that traditional models are more appropriate for studying circumstances in which *individual users*
adopt innovations as *autonomous* choices and for *personal*
use. However, the context in which organizations typically
operate at present is one in which the italicized terms above
are far less relevant than was once the case. In organizations,
the decision to adopt a technological innovation is not undertaken by individual users but is instead most often taken by an
authority figure, and individual employees are then mandated
to adopt the innovation. In addition, the technology is used
by a large number of employees throughout the organization
rather than being adopted for purely individual use.

Gallivan found major limitations in traditional models such
as the technology acceptance model (Davis 1989) and the diffusion of innovation theory (Rogers 1996). These models do
not mesh well in the sort of situations that Fichman (1992)
characterized as exhibiting "implementation complexity."
This complexity arises in organizational scenarios that require
high levels of coordination across multiple types of adopters
(Burton-Jones and Gallivan 2007). Traditional models cannot
conceptualize and analyze the gap between primary and secondary adoption in organizational settings, which are generally characterized by complex scenarios and authority-based
adoption (Cooper and Zmud 1990), because they were not
designed for that purpose. There is often an assimilation gap
(Fichman 1992) between the primary adoption decision and
secondary adoption, which involves the actual deployment or

implementation of the technology. Gallivan identified an additional shortcoming in traditional models that applies to circumstances in which adoption requires extensive, specialized training to overcome knowledge barriers to use.

These deficiencies in traditional models led Gallivan to propose an alternative, more comprehensive framework based on a hybrid model that combines both the processes of innovation adoption and relevant factors that mediate adoption at the organizational level. Because OSS adoption accurately describes the characteristics of secondary adoption and assimilation that were discussed above, this book derives its framework from the framework proposed by Gallivan (figure 2.1). This chapter discusses the individual components of the framework in greater detail and examines their relevance in an OSS context.

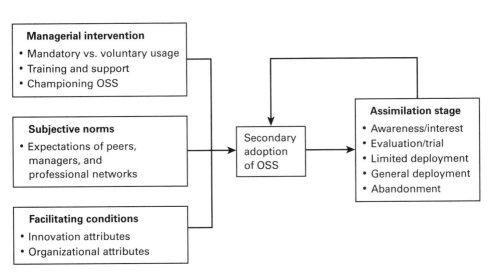

Figure 2.1
A framework for investigating OSS.

EXPLANATION OF THE FRAMEWORK IN AN OSS CONTEXT

Gallivan's model includes some principles from the theory of planned behavior (Ajzen 1985; Taylor and Todd 1995) that mediate between primary and secondary adoption. It specifically consists of two internal components, managerial interventions and subjective norms, that capture processes and factors related to organizational and individual actions and perceptions. A third external attribute included in this book's research framework, facilitating conditions, includes environmental factors that influence the diffusion of innovation within the organization is based largely on Rogers' (2003) innovation attributes and Orlikowski's (1993) organizational and individual attributes.

Managerial Intervention

Managerial intervention refers to actions taken and resources made available by management for the purpose of expediting secondary adoption. This includes issues such as deciding whether adoption is mandatory or voluntary, providing training and support, hiring new employees or consultants to act as mentors, and championing the OSS adoption initiative.

Management support is undoubtedly critical for radical, high-risk initiatives such as OSS deployment because it contravenes the traditional model in which ongoing support is legally guaranteed by a vendor. Indeed, management support is likely to become even more important in the future as OSS adoption moves beyond the domain of invisible infrastructure systems and into more visible, high-profile applications.

Championing OSS within the organization is a critical managerial intervention factor that is specifically relevant to

OSS adoption. This factor has been neglected in traditional technology adoption analyses because other sources of support are guaranteed (e.g., by vendors). This factor emerged as an important one in initial surveys of OSS adoption (Glynn, Fitzgerald, and Exton 2005).

Subjective Norms

Subjective norms concern how individuals believe their peers and coworkers expect them to behave in relation to technology. This can lead to enhanced efforts to learn about and adopt an innovation or to abandon a technology. This issue of behavioral expectation resonates with attributes of the innovation, such as compatibility and image.

Previous research has tended to conflate managerial intervention and subjective norms. Gallivan, however, argues cogently for the separation of the subjective factors from objectively determined factors. Subjective factors may largely concern perceptions but can be influential in the secondary adoption process.

From the perspective of values and norms, the ideology represented by OSS may have significant implications. The importance of ideological values in OSS has been well documented. Studies identify how adherence to an overarching OSS community ideology facilitates team effectiveness (Stewart and Gosain 2006). Similarly, the protracted and heated dispute that has persisted for several years among the Linux kernel development community concerning the use of a proprietary version control system (BitKeeper) represents an ideological crisis for many members of that community and has certainly influenced the choice of adoption and nonadoption of the technology (Shaikh 2006).

Facilitating Conditions: Attributes of the Innovation and Organization

Attributes of the Innovation

Rogers (Rogers 2003) identifies five key perceived attributes of an innovation that influence the outcome of the adoption process:

• *Relative advantage*   Relative advantage is the extent to which an innovation is perceived as being better than its precursor.

• *Compatibility*   Compatibility is the degree to which an innovation is perceived as being consistent with the existing values, norms, needs, and past experiences of potential adopters.

• *Complexity*   Complexity is the degree to which an innovation is perceived as being difficult to understand and use.

• *Trialability*   Trialability is the degree to which it is possible to experiment with an innovation.

• *Observability*   Observability is the degree to which the results of an innovation are visible to others.

In brief, Rogers suggests that innovations become diffused more quickly and successfully when they are readily *trialable*, have high *relative advantage* in comparison with the incumbent technology, are *compatible* with the preferred work practices and values of people, are not excessively *complex* to use, and where use is readily *observable* by others. These attributes have been confirmed in many studies. Additional relevant specific attributes of innovations, such as *image*, have been identified. Although this might be subsumed into Rogers' category of relative advantage, this attribute is worthy of isolation because it has been confirmed in several studies (Moore and Benbasat 1991; Tornatzky and Klein 1982).

Rogers' work is applicable to innovation in general, specifically in the category of IT adoption. The technology assessment model proposed by Davis (1989) has two central attributes—perceived usefulness and perceived ease of use. However, these are clearly subsumed within Rogers' attributes of relative advantage and complexity, respectively.

The above attributes are readily apparent within the context of OSS. In terms of relative advantage, compatibility, and complexity, many OSS products have been designed to replicate proprietary counterparts. The sense of familiarity that such products engender should mitigate adoption problems in relation to these attributes. On the other hand, the observability of OSS use is less obvious due to the strategy of replicating proprietary software. For example, it is quite difficult to distinguish between Microsoft Word, Excel, and PowerPoint and their respective OpenOffice counterparts, Writer, Calc, and Impress, merely by looking at users who work online using these applications.

Given that the acquisition of OSS products is usually a straightforward matter that is often as simple as a zero-cost download from a Web site, trialability is greatly facilitated in the specific case of OSS.

Image can be defined as the degree to which the adoption of an innovation enhances one's status. This emerged as a complex issue in relation to OSS. Studies of the motivations of OSS developers reveal that the intrinsic satisfaction of belonging to a meritocratic community in which talented developers can progress to become core developers is a motivating force for participation (e.g., Kuk 2006; Lakhani and Wolf 2005). From the user perspective, public administrations, particularly in Europe, have enthusiastically sought to deploy OSS because they view it as a positive initiative that frees them from the constraints of the proprietary software industry.[1] However, other reports have found that developers do not necessarily embrace open source (Zachary 2003). In addition, from the user perspective, there may be resistance to the use of open source products (van Reijswoud 2005). This suggests that the adoption and use of OSS may not be universally perceived as an image enhancer.

Organizational Attributes

As mentioned above, one criticism of innovation adoption literature is that it has focused narrowly on adoption at the individual level and has failed to focus on the organizational level and business contexts (Eveland and Tornatzky 1990; Swanson 1994). With this in mind, this book includes organizational factors in its framework.

Innovation researchers have identified several organizational attributes that may have a significant influence on the adoption process, including general attitude to risk, IT governance policies and standards in relation to software, and absorptive capacity.

Risk-averse industry sectors often exhibit a reluctance to engage with inherently risky implementations such as OSS, because they do not offer traditional legal comforts such as vendor-guaranteed telephone support hotlines and written maintenance contracts. However, European governments and public sector organizations, while generally risk averse, have turned out to be proactive in encouraging the adoption of OSS. Although there are risks associated with relatively unknown phenomena such as OSS implementation, institutional support for such initiatives can mitigate this concern.

In sectors that are highly regulated and in which interoperability is paramount, long-standing IT governance policies may exist in relation to IT infrastructure. These policies were often written in an era in which OSS solutions were not widely available and may mandate a proprietary software solution by default even though there is no compelling reason to do so. Thus, a particular proprietary software application may ironically appear to offer a de facto standard for interoperability (this is arguable, however, given that OSS is increasingly promoted as a solution that can guarantee interoperability). Some industry sectors may have bulk-purchasing agreements with proprietary software vendors. In addition, software packages in some industries must comply with standard architectures. In the health sector, the Health Level Seven (HL7) standard for intersystem/organization messaging and the Digital Imaging and Communications in Medicine (DICOM) standard for image management are common examples.

Absorptive capacity refers to an organization's ability to recognize the value of new information, absorb it, and subsequently leverage it productively (Cohen and Levinthal 1990). Absorptive capacity is relevant for OSS adoption in general. The ever-increasing number of OSS applications that continue to appear in the marketplace represent a significant knowledge challenge that needs to be overcome. For example, an organization needs to know what applications exist, which applications are most viable, how well applications are supported, what functionality applications offer, and how applications can be integrated with other OSS or proprietary applications. Indeed, developers have referred to the "exhilarating succession of problem-solving challenges" when installing OSS products (Sanders 1998). Given that there is no tried-and-true roadmap that indicates a clearly outlined series of steps that will guarantee successful deployment, organizations cannot expect to have sufficiently lengthy experience with OSS deployment that will guarantee success. Thus, the process of OSS implementation is clearly one in which absorptive capacity can play a crucial role.

Secondary Adoption Process and Assimilation Stage
As mentioned above, secondary adoption refers to the stage of the organizational implementation process in which individuals throughout an organization adopt an innovation. This includes when and how an innovation is adopted, what obstacles are encountered, and how these factors influence the outcome and the degree of organizational assimilation.

Given that technology acquisition and deployment represent different types of assimilation events, the level or degree of assimilation can be viewed as a staged process, from awareness/interest through general deployment. This book proposes the following adoption scenarios:

• *Awareness/interest*   Key decision makers in an organization become aware of OSS and become actively committed to learning more about it.

• *Evaluation/trial*   An organization has acquired specific OSS products and has initiated evaluations or trials.

• *Limited deployment*   An organization has established a program of regular but limited use of OSS products.

• *General deployment*   An organization uses OSS products for at least one large mission-critical system.

• *Abandonment*   An organization has discontinued the live use of OSS products.

Gallivan's framework includes the six stages of IT assimilation defined in the model of Cooper and Zmud (1990): the initiation (preadoption stage), the adoption stage itself, and four postadoption stages (adaptation, acceptance, routinization, and infusion). In order to preserve the dynamic perspective of Cooper and Zmud (1990), this book uses a staged evolution that is in keeping with the assimilation stages suggested by Fichman and Kemerer (1997). Its set of assimilation stages differs from those listed above but nevertheless maintains an overall logical correspondence with the Cooper and Zmud (1990) stages. The book's five stages also take into account the issue of trust and attitude regarding OSS. In particular, it considers the initial stage of awareness or interest in OSS that typically arises among both decision makers and employees. OSS assimilation was characterized by considering the extent of adoption within the organization as a whole rather than individual acceptance of the technology, in keeping with the desire to investigate secondary adoption. Finally, the stage of OSS abandonment was included, which was not part of Gallivan's framework, assuming that, when use is mandatory, abandonment is not possible. There are a number of examples of OSS abandonment in the literature, however (Thurston 2006; Turner 2005; Niccolai 2005; McCue 2004), and evidence of abandonment appears in the case studies presented in chapters 3 through 7.

This framework is used in subsequent chapters to analyze the OSS adoption process in five case studies.

3
Hibernia Hospital

INTRODUCTION

Ireland's Hibernia Hospital[1] employs about 3,000 staff members directly. Hibernia's IT budget, as is the case with many other organizations worldwide, has contracted significantly since 2000. For example, in 2003, Hibernia faced an overall budgetary shortfall of more than $23 million. Hibernia was thus faced with the choice of either reducing the overall level of service in order to cope with cost restrictions or implementing radical innovations as a means of developing less costly alternatives. As a result, Hibernia began to investigate what was available in the open source marketplace. The IT staff at Hibernia extensively researched various OSS products during a six-month period. The quality of the exchanges on Source-Forge and Slashdot were sufficient to convince Hibernia's IT manager that OSS merited further investigation. Some direct experimentation with downloaded OSS programs helped convince him that the risks involved were acceptable.

This chapter focuses on the adoption process for two OSS applications at Hibernia—the StarOffice desktop suite, whose deployment was ultimately unsuccessful and an open source email platform, which was ultimately deployed in a successful manner.

STAROFFICE DESKTOP SUITE

StarOffice is available from Sun Microsystems, a company that is also the driving force behind OpenOffice. Some proprietary software is bundled with StarOffice, which prevents it from being offered on the same terms as the pure OSS OpenOffice with which it shares a common code base. Hibernia decided to implement StarOffice so that it could then purchase support from Sun. This was considered important for mitigating the risk when the company embarked on radical new initiatives such as OSS deployment.

In February 2002, Hibernia began the rollout of StarOffice 5.2 desktop suite. This deployment was quite problematic for users and the technical staff, but this was believed to be largely due to problems in version 5.2 of StarOffice. In September 2002, StarOffice 6.0 was deployed with support from Sun. This deployment was also troublesome; Hibernia's IT manager pursued a thin client strategy based on the concept that all of the applications should be downloaded from the network whenever this was practical. The StarOffice package was initially loaded onto a single Linux server, but this server soon became overwhelmed, and it was then clustered in order to sustain a dual-server strategy. Users continued to lose network connections unpredictably. This increased the level of frustration and tension among the workforce, which was heavily dependent on these tools. The IT manager conceded that "we stuck with the network solution too long. It was only after a series of ferocious encounters with users—and with my own staff—that I recognized that we had to shift."

StarOffice was reinstalled on the desktop for those who wanted it, which improved the situation, according to technical staff. In November 2003, Hibernia installed StarOffice 7.0. This version solved many existing problems, and the IT manager reported that there were no open bug reports in Hibernia for StarOffice 7.0. Nevertheless, user perceptions of the StarOffice system appear to have been damaged irreparably.

EMAIL PLATFORM

Prior to the move to OSS, Hibernia's email system was a proprietary system that had a 500-user license limit. This limit had been reached, and the IT manager had to refuse requests for new email accounts. Hibernia initially adopted the SuSE email application, an open source email platform supported by Novell, after the acquisition of SuSE Linux. Although the SuSE email application did not limit the number of user email accounts, once the system reached about 700 user email accounts, the system became prone to problems, such as hanging and crashing on a frequent basis. Hibernia paid a consultant a one-off fee to implement the SuSE application initially. As with StarOffice, Hibernia sought to establish a support contract for SuSE email. When Hibernia experienced problems in attempting to secure such support, it began to search for an alternative open source email platform, and a multiproduct open source email platform was established. It consisted of the Postfix mail transport agent, the OpenLDAP directory access protocol service, the SpamAssassin mail filter, and the SquirrelMail email client. After some initial problems with integration, this mixed architecture emerged as an extremely stable and scalable email solution. Given that there were no license-imposed constraints on the number of users, Hibernia initiated a policy that allowed all staff members to have email accounts. Hibernia's IT staff members were also able to add functionality, meaning that they could reroute emails to mobile phones and PDAs. This capability, together with the filtering capability of SpamAssassin, resulted in the email platform being received very favorably among the general user base. The system scaled successfully and was able to support more than 3,000 email accounts. In addition, the system scope was expanded to incorporate certificate-based external email access for about 350 authorized users. The IT manager believes that "it would be unthinkable and completely unacceptable" to revert to a 500-user license again.

ANALYSIS OF OSS ADOPTION IN HIBERNIA HOSPITAL

This section discusses the different implementation trajectories for both open source applications within Hibernia using the framework described in chapter 2.

Managerial Intervention

Mandatory versus Voluntary Usage
The decision to move to OSS had the full support of the CEO of Hibernia, primarily because no other alternatives were available, given the cuts in the IT capital budget. The use of StarOffice was regarded as mandatory. This had significant negative implications. As Hibernia's secretarial manager put it, "We did not think that StarOffice had been given to us as

a bonus. Rather, we felt that Microsoft Office had been taken away."

Although the move to StarOffice was mandated, not everyone was obliged to migrate. Hibernia consists of numerous largely autonomous units that operate independently and raise research funds to support their activities. Among these independent units, about 120 users chose to ignore the move to StarOffice. These users typically had sufficient funds to remain independent of central IT support. The IT manager, however, informed these users that this would have consequences in the sense that they would have to take responsibility for ensuring that the hardware they use is upgraded, provide resources for future maintenance upgrades, and so forth.

The issue of mandatory usage did not arise in the case of the email platform suite. Hibernia offered an additional service in the form of email access to those who had sought but had been unable to obtain email access in the past. Thus, the email platform was implemented in the context of voluntary user demand rather than there being the perception of a policy of management-mandated usage.

Training and Support

The secretarial manager was critical of the manner in which StarOffice had been initially implemented. In her opinion, there was no effective buy-in process. The small pilot group included only one secretary during the initial trial. This was inadequate, given that the most active users of StarOffice would be the numerous secretaries who worked at Hibernia. The secretarial manager suggested that "StarOffice was sold as the same thing as Microsoft Office. A two-page brochure was provided and it was suggested that no training would be needed really."

However, even though StarOffice and Microsoft Office are essentially functionally equivalent, the menus are constructed differently, and the terminology is slightly different. Thus, commonly used options, such as Print Preview or Track Changes, have different labels or appear in different submenus and have different keystroke shortcuts. This contributed to a greater feeling of unfamiliarity and incompatibility than was probably warranted, given the numerous similarities between the applications.

Further compounding the problems was the fact that when Hibernia initiated StarOffice implementation in 2002, very little training material was available. Thus, a great deal of material had to be prepared internally, which increased the workload of the IT staff and trainers. Given the problems with the deployment of earlier versions of StarOffice, a training and awareness program was created in order to ensure that the user community would be briefed on the new features in StarOffice 7.0. While this would address user perceptions in relation to issues of complexity, relative advantage, and compatibility, it was insufficient to overcome the highly negative perceptions associated with StarOffice in Hibernia, despite the fact that Hibernia had no unresolved problem reports for StarOffice 7.0.

There was no specific training or extra support in the case of email, so any differences between the original proprietary application and the subsequent OSS application would not have been perceived as being problematic. However, the user base for email grew from 500 to over 3,000, and the vast majority of the users did not have an existing workplace email application that they would have needed to unlearn. In addition, there were no alternative email applications elsewhere in Hibernia against which unfavorable comparisons could be made, which helped to minimize this potential problem.

Subjective Norms

In the case of StarOffice, the user base perceived usage as being mandatory for those who did not have the resources for an alternative. This led to feelings of resentment, which were quick to emerge when problems became apparent. Interestingly, departments and users who were able to remain on the proprietary platform were envied by their colleagues instead of being seen as renegades. The secretarial manager described it as follows: "You meet people and hear that they are using Microsoft, and immediately you ask them how they managed to do that."

One key complaint from administrative staff members in Hibernia who migrated to the StarOffice platform was their fear of becoming de-skilled in relation to their employment prospects if they were not skilled at using popular proprietary applications. In fact, users readily admitted that they would have preferred to not have made the switch from the proprietary desktop systems to OSS. In addition, there remained resentment in some quarters concerning the move to OSS systems. Some staff members felt "short-changed" and believed that their work had been undervalued if they were asked to use OSS systems, which cost less than proprietary systems.

Facilitating Conditions

Innovation Attributes

Chapter 2 discussed several innovation attributes that previous research has shown influence the adoption of innovations.

This section discusses the attributes that are most relevant to the OSS adoption in Hibernia—image, relative advantage, trialability, and observability.

Image

Possibly the most significant issue for StarOffice was that it had rapidly acquired a negative image. Despite the improvements that were available in newer versions of the software, this negative image persisted. One user admitted that when StarOffice was proposed, there was a widespread perception that this was a cheap and antiquated package from *Jurassic Park* with limited functionality. This user was genuinely surprised to hear that StarOffice was a modern application that was under active development. This negative view was confirmed by an informatics nurse who suggested that StarOffice ran into "bad publicity from the outset."

The significance of this perception was that no other hospital in the country had chosen to implement an OSS desktop at the time. The secretarial manager suggested that the budget-cutting rationale behind the implementation of StarOffice resulted in it being perceived as a "poor man's Microsoft," and the preconceived expectation was that the software would be problematic.

It was suggested that one negative effect of StarOffice was that it might have been seen as the underlying cause of an increased level of absenteeism and stress-related sick leave, according to the occupation health department. However, there was no rigorous analysis of employee absences that supported this contention. The StarOffice image has become notorious within Hibernia to the extent that during meetings in which new IT projects are discussed, managers have expressed the hope that new projects will not turn out to be "another StarOffice." The negative image of StarOffice extends beyond Hibernia. One user described emailing an attachment that had been saved in StarOffice's proprietary format by default to an external colleague. This colleague was unable to open the attachment and emailed a response saying that the attachment was in "StarOffice gobbledygook."

In sharp contrast, the email platform has not acquired a negative image. While there were problems during the implementation phase of SuSE email, these problems were quickly overcome when an alternative email system was implemented. In addition, these problems manifested only when more than 200 additional users were given email access. Thus, there was no sense that the user service had been downgraded in any way. This resonates with the relative advantage issue that is discussed in the next section.

Relative Advantage
The initial problems that were experienced with StarOffice led users to believe that the original proprietary system was superior to StarOffice. There were several problems, particularly with Impress, the StarOffice equivalent of Microsoft PowerPoint. An informatics nurse described it as follows: "I have seen people crying because of Impress. One day I was working on a presentation which I was due to give at 8:30 the following morning. At 5:30 p.m. I checked it and it had become just one blank sheet. I had to go home and recreate it from memory in PowerPoint."

The IT manager also recalled giving a seminar on OSS at an IT conference attended by several hundred delegates, and his Impress presentation stalled. This was an unhappy experience, and the software on which public presentations depend is not an area in which problems will be tolerated for long. This issue is interesting because there are only a small number of users who must deliver presentations at Hibernia, so the problems that were experienced with Impress were not particularly widespread. Nevertheless, users appeared to very readily empathize with the negative scenario of the problems that were experienced with public presentations.

StarOffice and Microsoft Office are essentially equivalent functionally, but there are some differences that were cited as a reason to not migrate to StarOffice. For example, the finance department cited the row number limit in StarOffice Calc, which is less than is the case for Microsoft Excel, as a reason for not migrating.

However, when things settled down, particularly after the installation of StarOffice 7.0, a number of benefits offered by the OSS solution became evident. For example, one benefit is the capacity of StarOffice to exploit its built-in XML capabilities. This is a powerful feature that allows documents to be structured in such a way that processing logic is built into different sections of the document; for example, an on-line personnel form request can be automatically routed to the human resources department for processing. This is a feature was not offered in the previous versions of Hibernia's proprietary desktop applications.

The StarOffice suite included an option that allowed for the creation of output in .pdf format, which was not available in the Microsoft Office implementation once used in Hibernia. Several interviewees mentioned this as an improvement. Although the StarOffice Impress application was clearly the most notable problem, there was support for the other

StarOffice applications. One interviewee expressed a distinct preference for StarOffice's Calc over Microsoft Office Excel. However, such perceptions did not scale into an overarching perception of the relative advantage of StarOffice over the proprietary system it replaced.

Regarding the relative advantage of SuSE email, Hibernia could satisfy additional requests for email accounts, which was an improved form of service. There were significant problems regarding the use of SuSE email to start, but these were short-lived problems that Hibernia was able to overcome rapidly by implementing an alternative OSS email suite. Again, these problems only occurred after the addition of more than 200 additional email accounts, so there was no real perception that the OSS system was operating at a disadvantage. The option of replacing StarOffice was not possible. Although the problems were ironed out in subsequent installations of StarOffice, the perception of StarOffice led to it being viewed with suspicion.

Some users were unaware of alternative email applications that were in use in other departments at that time. In addition, users typically did not have an alternative email application at home, whereas Microsoft Office users often had that product installed on their home computers.

Trialability
Trialabilty was a key issue in Hibernia's OSS deployment. During the initial stage, Hibernia's IT staff was able to download and experiment with several OSS applications of potential interest. Given the budget situation, this zero-cost exercise was important. When Hibernia experienced problems with the SuSE email implementation, IT staff members experimented

with a range of alternative OSS email applications and implemented a successful and scalable email solution in short order.

This mode of OSS implementation continued. When Hibernia selected an online e-learning system, it tried out a number of OSS e-learning systems before selecting the one that appeared to best meet its needs.

Interestingly, this easy trialability appears to have implications for the training and support process, because less attention was paid to it. If it had been a high-cost initiative, it probably would have had a higher profile within the organization, and, consequently, more attention would have been given to implementation issues, such as pilot testing, training, and support. The IT manager summarized the dilemma: "If you have a product which costs $1 million—it may seem appropriate to spend $500K on consulting. However, if the product costs nothing—then spending $500K somehow seems to be a more difficult decision to take—yet the saving is still $1 million." Hibernia learned this lesson and went on to develop a more comprehensive user awareness and training package to support the implementation of StarOffice 7.0.

Observability
Rogers suggests that the extent to which the results of an innovation are observable by others will affect its rate of diffusion. However, given that Hibernia sought to achieve the smoothest possible transition, the goal was to minimize and downplay the differences between StarOffice and Microsoft Office in order to ensure that the two programs would be perceived as being identical. This is usually not difficult in an OSS context because applications are usually designed to replicate the functionality of proprietary systems. Thus, instead

of attempting to publicly trumpet the use of StarOffice as progressive and desirable, the emphasis was on downplaying the issue of observability. Given the negative image of OSS in Hibernia, there was a conscious decision to not identify IT applications as being open source. Thus, the issue did not arise in the case of the email application. In a similar manner, when Hibernia later implemented an OSS e-learning system, the reality that the systems being trialed were open source was deliberately downplayed.

Organizational Attributes

Absorptive Capacity

Hibernia's absorptive capacity in relation to OSS adoption was important. The IT manager accepted that the initial roll-out of StarOffice was poorly conceived, and Hibernia learned that it needed to act in a different manner during subsequent implementations of OSS. The OSS path involved risks, given that ongoing product support would not be provided in the usual manner. There was a need to completely rethink support strategy. Hibernia had previously purchased support from a competent third-party provider. With OSS, this option still existed, but there was a significant difference in expectations regarding OSS, given that support essentially derived from a series of bulletin boards that were complemented with external consultancy during the early stages until Hibernia became fully competent.

It helped that a number of key staff, particularly in the computer operations department, rapidly adapted to the new OSS environment. The IT manager described the operations team as the "leaders in the overall adoption of OSS." Most of the overall OSS search selection and implementation was actually carried out by the hospital staff. This necessarily involved learning and experimentation. As staff confidence and familiarity with OSS products increased, the learning cycles correspondingly shortened. It helped that Hibernia already had experience with UNIX applications to draw on. The transition was thus not as radical as would have been the case if staff experience had been simply based on graphical-user-interface-enabled (GUI-enabled) systems administration. In the words of the Linux systems administrator, "We are not afraid of the command line interface."

Evidence of increased absorptive capacity in relation to open source is readily evident in the email application deployments. When Hibernia encountered insurmountable problems in relation to the open source SuSE email application, the IT staff quickly sourced an alternative suite of email applications. This integration of an entire suite of disparate open source email applications into a single integrated email platform represented a significant technological challenge, from initially identifying suitable applications to integrating them into an overall working application.

CONCLUSIONS

Table 3.1 summarizes the differences in the deployment process for the OSS desktop and email applications within Hibernia.

Two key issues were trialability and absorptive capacity, because these factors facilitated OSS adoption. Trialability of OSS ensured that Hibernia could experiment with OSS applications and be reasonably confident that the OSS applications that were available could meet its needs. In addition, when problems occurred, as in the case of the initial OSS email implementation, an alternative could be found to solve the problem. However, while trialability facilitates the primary adoption of OSS, it is the absorptive capacity that ensures that the best OSS candidates get selected and are successfully integrated and implemented, which thereby facilitate successful secondary adoption.

Other interlinked elements, such as voluntary versus mandatory adoption and the image of the innovation, manifested themselves in a manner that impeded the assimilation of OSS within Hibernia.

First, by being perceived as mandatory due to the need to cut costs, the adoption of StarOffice was perceived as reactive. When it emerged that some "more privileged" users could opt out of the move, this two-tier scenario significantly contributed to the negative image StarOffice acquired. When problems occurred, the image problem fostered a disproportionately negative perception of StarOffice, despite the program offering certain extra functionality. A steady state with no open bug reports was eventually attained following the implementation of StarOffice 7.0. The email application shared a similar deployment trajectory because it also faced problems during the initial stages, and these were later overcome. The OSS email system had advantages over the original proprietary system. The critical difference was that the move to email was not seen as a top-down mandate, because users had to request an email account. Furthermore, there were no coworkers who were using an alternative system that might have been perceived as privileged.

Table 3.1
OSS Deployment within Hibernia

	StarOffice desktop	Email platform
Managerial intervention		
Mandatory vs. voluntary usage	Usage was seen as mandatory for those who could not afford to maintain a proprietary alternative.	Access to email application was provided upon request, so usage was not perceived as being mandatory.
Training and support	Differences between OSS and proprietary systems were downplayed. There was a low level of initial training using material developed in-house.	No specialized training was necessary, because there was no incumbent proprietary system to unlearn.
Subjective Norms		
User perceptions	Mandatory usage for users who could not afford to maintain proprietary system led to StarOffice being perceived as inferior. Staff feared being de-skilled if they used OSS, and they believed that their work would be undervalued if they used "cheap" OSS. Those who opted out of the migration to StarOffice were envied rather than resented.	More than 2,500 additional user requests for email accounts were satisfied. The email platform was uniformly perceived as beneficial. There was no alternative email system against which unfavorable comparisons could be made.
Facilitating conditions: Innovation attributes		
Image	StarOffice was seen as a cheap and antiquated *Jurassic Park* option for the disadvantaged. There was a widespread negative image of StarOffice both within and external to Hibernia.	Email access was seen by many as a new privilege that had not been previously available.

Table 3.1
(continued)

	StarOffice desktop	Email platform
Relative advantage	Problems and instability led to StarOffice being perceived as inferior. Impress problems were cited. Benefits of StarOffice were not widely appreciated.	Email was a new application for the majority of users, and there was no basis for comparison with older products. Problems with intermediate SuSE email were quickly resolved, and new functionality (routing of email to PDAs) was appreciated.
Trialability	Trialability was important but limited due to lack of alternative OSS desktop suites.	Trialability was critical given that Hibernia experimented with a number of OSS email applications.
Observability	StarOffice and Microsoft Office appear identical on casual observation. Thus, OSS usage is not readily apparent and observable.	Observability was downplayed due to negative image of OSS. This was not a major issue because no alternative email application was in use that could be used for comparison purposes.
Facilitating conditions: Organizational attributes		
Absorptive capacity	This capacity was important because OSS represents a new model of software acquisition, implementation, and support. Prior learning was evident in implementation of StarOffice 7.0.	This capacity was highly relevant because the first OSS email application had to be replaced with a suite of individual OSS email applications in a novel mixed architecture. There was a high knowledge burden in selecting the right applications to include in this architecture and configuring them to work successfully together.

The issue of observability emerged during the Hibernia OSS adoption process. It was not obvious at a casual glance whether a user was using StarOffice or Microsoft Office. In the case of email, the vast majority of users acquired access to email for the first time using StarOffice at Hibernia. This highlighted the observability issue, because users who were sending email had not done so previously. This led to additional requests for email accounts. However, because open source had a negative image as a result of the StarOffice experience, Hibernia sought to downplay the reality that proposed applications, such as e-learning, were OSS applications.

The most striking point in this case was not that any individual factors were critical but rather that the interaction among the holistic configuration of elements was a significant influence on OSS implementation.

4
Südtiroler Gemeindenverband

INTRODUCTION

The Südtiroler Gemeindenverband (SGV), or Consorzio dei Comuni della Provincia di Bolzano (<http://www.gvcc.net>), is a consortium founded fifty years ago that serves 116 municipalities, 8 social service offices, and about 30 offices by providing social support in the Italian province of Bolzano-Bozen. Most of the municipalities have two to three employees and have little by way of IT skills. The province is bilingual (speaking Italian and German), and all of the official documents are written in the two languages (often using the two-column style).

The SGV's major task is to formulate policies regarding the usage of the available hardware and software and manage the central servers of the consortium. In particular, the consortium is responsible for selecting, developing, and installing hardware and software for public services within a radius of about one hundred kilometers of the mountainous province of Bolzano-Bozen. Half of the SGV's employees work in IT, coordinating the municipalities' IT departments and supporting about 3,500 personal computers (PCs) and 180 servers, routers, and switches.

SGV has a star structure. Each municipality pays a yearly fee for the SGV services. Some of the larger municipalities run their own IT departments, but the smaller municipalities are completely dependent upon the central service of SGV.

This large and varied structure of the municipalities demands a well-defined strategy for the standardization of the procedures, coordination of SGV with the municipalities, and alignment of the underlying IT infrastructure with respect to the local autonomy of each member. Thus, the major mission of SGV is to create and maintain the standards and quality of the services across the municipalities of the province. Maintaining such a network requires SGV to rely on several local vendors and to base its infrastructure on various proprietary software products. In 1998, the costs for IT became so high that SGV decided to explore alternative ways to optimize public expenditures.

The first alternative involved the back-office migration of servers to Linux. The migration achieved general deployment in April 2001. It was successful in the sense that costs were reduced and kept under control, although it required hiring skilled people to maintain the system. The client side of the information system remained based upon proprietary solutions, however. Switching to a new software schema on the client side was considered too risky at that time.

Convincing the management of SGV to adopt OSS on an extensive basis involved a series of favorable circumstances that began in 2002. The computer science faculty of the local university published several studies showing that no performance degradation resulted from moving from Microsoft

Office to OpenOffice (Rossi, Russo, and Succi 2007; Rossi, Russo, and Succi 2006a; Russo, Succi, and Zuliani 2003). The computer science faculty later coordinated a European project that promoted the adoption of open data standards and OSS in public administrations (COSPA project[1]). SGV took an active part in this project by supplying data and practical experience. Meanwhile, the public high schools of the province adopted Linux and OpenOffice for all student PCs under the umbrella name of the FUSS[2] project.

In this context, SGV began the migration of its desktop systems at the end of 2003, and this process reached general deployment in 2004. Software for personal productivity was tested and installed gradually in the majority of municipalities.

OSS IN SGV

As mentioned above, SGV adopted its first open source application in 1998 and ramped up its OSS activity in 2003 when it migrated to OpenOffice.

The OSS adoption pattern can be traced by examining SGV's experiences with three software products—server-side operating system, Linux server; desktop system, OpenOffice; and groupware, Group E. Table 4.1 shows their dates of introduction, the levels of assimilation at the end of 2005, and the dates when these levels were achieved.

SGV's IT staff installed all three OSS products. About one month was required for the server-side installations and setup, but installing the office applications took only about ten minutes per PC to remotely deploy. The IT staff wrote scripts that facilitated the remote installation of the office suites. In many of the municipalities, the desktop migration required on-site

Table 4.1
Key OSS Applications at SGV (End of 2005)

OSS product	Date of adoption	Current level of assimilation (end of 2005)	Date when current level was achieved
Operating system (Linux server)	1998	General deployment	April 2001
Desktop system (OpenOffice)	2003	General deployment	2004
Groupware (Group-E)	2003	Limited deployment	2004

setup and the geographic distribution of the municipalities' sites resulted in significant travel expenses. The groupware software product was designed and developed by a local company. As requested in the contract, the product was released with the open license and the company guaranteed maintenance and support. The product interface was designed in such a way that the end users did not perceive any changes. However, at the end of 2005, the groupware product had yet to reach general deployment due to the internal policies of some of the municipalities.

The introduction of the OSS did not require any new hardware or infrastructure upgrades, and regular hardware updates continued as usual.

Operating Systems (Server-Side)—Linux
Linux is the most prominent example of free software and open source development at SGV. SGV installed Linux on 238 servers. Two out of three of these systems were file servers, while the others played a variety of roles, including a database

Table 4.2
OSS Adopted at SGV for the Operating System (Server-Side)

Function	Software
File server	Samba (<http://www.samba.org>)
Directory service	OpenLDAP (<http://www.openldap.org>)
Proxy server	Squid (<http://www.squid-cache.org>)
Firewall	Iptables (<http://www.netfilter.org>)

server, dynamic host configuration protocol (DHCP) server, proxy server, firewall, and lightweight directory access protocol (LDAP) server.

Every Linux server was customized by adding specific open source packages, such as Samba, Squid, iptables, and OpenLDAP (table 4.2).

Desktop Applications—OpenOffice

The municipalities of the province of Bolzano-Bozen deployed OpenOffice (<http://www.OpenOffice.org>) on a large scale. At the end of 2004, the application ran on 2,829 PCs. Employees could initially choose to use either OpenOffice or Microsoft Office.

These organizations employ two languages in their operations, and the existence of document templates in both Italian and German presented a problem for SGV. It therefore developed its own data format converter and replicated old templates in the OpenOffice format.

This process revealed shortcomings in two of the components of OpenOffice. The version of Base[3] used by SGV lacks many of the functions that are found in Microsoft Access, and some of the graphical features of Microsoft Excel are better than those offered by Calc.[4]

Although employees could choose between OpenOffice and Microsoft Office, some of the documents for internal use were only available in the open source format. The election templates, for example, were created with OpenOffice. This was part of the consortium's strategy to promote the diffusion of open data standards. By the end of 2005, at least twelve municipalities, which were using a total of 344 PCs, had completely migrated to OpenOffice and had uninstalled Microsoft Office.

As of May 2005, OpenOffice was installed on more than 2,500 workstations. About 400 users in more than 20 municipalities work with the OSS suite exclusively. SGV offered ad hoc training with the installation of the new office suites. Each municipality chose whether it wanted to participate. In early 2006, twenty-three municipalities had installed this software on all of their workstations, sixty-four had performed a partial installation, and twenty-nine had not yet installed the application.

The introduction of OpenOffice provided new functionalities that were perceived to be beneficial by nonexpert users. In order to encourage adoption, during the transition most of the document templates were upgraded, extended, and enhanced in order to provide additional functionalities beyond those offered with the old version of Microsoft Office templates. Furthermore, OpenOffice could open Microsoft Office documents and support open data standards, enabling end users to work with more data formats. OpenOffice could also open old Microsoft documents that were no longer supported by the proprietary format.

The negative effects reported by the end users related primarily to the spreadsheet application Calc of OpenOffice and the OpenOffice Base. The former application provided few of the graphical features of Microsoft Excel, and the latter application lacked many of the features that Microsoft Access offered. No specific shortcoming was reported for the presentation application Impress, possibly because it was not used by the majority of the users.

Groupware—Group-E

Group-E (<http://www.group-e.info>) is an open source platform for communication, organization, and management for working teams. This program was developed by a local software company and can be applied in different fields. It has been adopted by several public and private sector organizations in the province. It is written in PHP and uses the open source MySQL software as a back-end database.

Group-E was installed in 30 municipalities and had 587 users by the end of 2005. The user interface of Group-E's communication module was modeled on the system it replaced. This guaranteed the highest possible acceptance of the new application. The majority of users did not perceive any major difference in comparison with the previous software program.

ANALYSIS OF OSS ADOPTION IN SGV

The following sections describe the adoption of the previously mentioned OSS products in the SGV consortium according to the framework described in chapter 2.

Managerial Intervention

The management of SGV had four strategic reasons for experimenting with OSS and migrating from proprietary products:

1. Limiting public expenditures. Financial constraints were not an issue, and there was no sense of urgency about reducing the costs of software, but the money saved by using OSS nevertheless could be used for other purposes. The change also had an ethical dimension: saving public money represented efficient management of the res publica.

2. Achieving independence from vendors. Most of the consortium's municipalities are unwilling to spend much on updates for their desktop computers and servers. SGV chose solutions that do not require frequent upgrades and has adapted tools to run on old hardware.

3. Giving citizens the opportunity to use open formats and free software.

4. Adhering to the promotion of OSS and standards by the Italian government.

In order to achieve these strategic objectives, SGV's IT management allocated time to search for and analyze alternative OSS solutions. Testing the selected software added two to three months to the timeline for the introduction of the operating system and added about one month to the timeline for the introduction of OpenOffice and the Group-E product. Over the long term, however, this approach resulted in an improvement of the overall performance of the systems at no additional expense.

Mandatory versus Voluntary Usage

The deployment of the Linux operating system on the server-side did not cause major problems or resistance. The management made the decision, and the migration was conducted rapidly. Existing and newly hired IT employees were enthusiastic about the change and were prepared to put in extra effort to support it.

The migration to OpenOffice initially created some resistance. The application was used by all of the employees, and many nonexpert users found the migration unnecessary. This initial adverse attitude was exacerbated by some of the negative outcomes produced by the first pilot implementation of OpenOffice. This project concerned a single municipality that volunteered for the experiment. Local technicians who lacked appropriate training were unable to solve technical problems related to certain instability issues of OpenOffice 1.0.1, and the SGV software experts were slow to respond because the pilot implementation period coincided with the Christmas break.

The first reactions of the municipalities to the new office suite varied in proportion to the size of those municipalities. The small municipalities that depended directly on the IT support of SGV were generally more willing to learn how to use OpenOffice, despite some instability and the flaws in version 1.0.1. Some of the larger municipalities that had internal IT departments exhibited substantially more resistance to the change because they perceived the migration to be more of an intrusion than a benefit.

The results of the pilot project initially disoriented the IT management of SGV. Fortunately, a series of positive events followed, and the management of SGV continued the adoption of OSS:

• The COSPA project[2] studied the impact of OSS in public administrations and showed that it was highly beneficial.

• A series of studies conducted by the computer science faculty of the Free University of Bozen-Bolzano showed that no performance degradation was incurred by moving from Microsoft Office to OpenOffice (Russo, Braghin, Gasperi, Sillitti, and Succi 2005; Succi and Zuliani 2004; Russo, Succi, and Zuliani 2003).

• The new and "almost Word-like" version 2.0 of OpenOffice was released.

• The FUSS project[3] involved the introduction of OpenOffice in public schools of the province.

SGV participated in the COSPA project and conducted the desktop software migration under the project's umbrella. During the project, a training manual for the most recent version of OpenOffice was created and made available to the employees of SGV and associated municipalities.[5] SGV learned from the experience of the pilot project. It revised its deployment plan, adding an initial training course for each municipality and hiring a training specialist who traveled to each municipality.

SGV also encouraged the adoption of OpenOffice by upgrading, extending, and enhancing document templates. It provided users with more functionality than the previous Microsoft Office templates had offered.

Management support for OSS started to produce some benefits in 2006. By the beginning of 2006, all of the IT staff and about 70% of the administrative offices were using open source applications; a small number used OSS exclusively—a combination of Linux and OpenOffice—while all of the others used a combination of Windows and OpenOffice.

Training and Support

As mentioned above, at the beginning of the migration project, few people were given proper OSS training. Some of the

IT personnel—about ten people—had received training for Linux and email servers. These people had prior experience with Novell operating systems, which proved to be a useful background for Linux adoption. Three more weeks of training were subsequently provided to the other six members of the IT staff.

As noted, the server-side migration was successfully completed. This encouraged the management to extend the transition to the office applications in all of the municipalities. Unfortunately, the results of the server-side migration were overestimated. The motivation, the enthusiasm, and the previous experience of the IT team had driven the success of the migration. Under these conditions, short-term training was sufficient and the need for specific training for a nonexpert user was not considered to be crucial for OpenOffice implementation. Therefore, SGV initially relied solely upon the experience of the SGV and local IT staff to implement the deployment of OSS in all of the municipalities. This level of training turned out to be insufficient during the first pilot project. As noted above, the municipalities' staff was unable to cope with certain aspects of the instability of the OpenOffice version and with certain features (e.g., the two-language style) of the application. This convinced SGV to invest in training for novice OpenOffice users.

In total, about 2,500 employees were trained over a two-month period. The training was delivered in several ways. If a municipality had an IT center, one day of training was provided to all personnel. SGV's IT staff made regular visits to the municipalities and offered on-site assistance. The consortium distributed product documentation through its intranet. A help desk was made available for one hour a day at the beginning of the migration process. SGV administrators offered remote support via virtual network computing (VNC)[6] tools for two hours a day. An additional trainer was hired and external consultants provided advice on Linux and other server-side software.

SGV also introduced a general training course in word processing open to all employees. This was done to emphasize how end users could tailor and customize the most useful features of OpenOffice. For example, employees were shown how to: use styles in writing documents, format the styles rapidly, write documents in two languages using multiple columns, and write documents for multiple recipients. Thus, as the transition to OpenOffice progressed, the employees learned to compare the capabilities of the new application with generic word-processing functions. This training continues to be provided on a regular basis in SGV and in the municipalities of the province.

Championing OSS Initiatives

The management of SGV has championed the OSS initiative since the initial stages of adoption. This was based on the knowledge that the greater the number of OSS users, the greater the software cost savings would be.

Furthermore, an individual's ideology was important at SGV. The chief information officer of SGV had championed OSS since the early stages of the migration. He promoted the open ideology inside and outside SGV in various ways. For example, he coordinated the participation of SGV in the European project COSPA as a means of convincing the municipalities of the benefits of OSS, and he participated in interviews with local and national media in order to disseminate information about the SGV experience outside the organization.

Subjective Norms

Aside from the IT specialists, most of the employees of the municipalities supported by SGV initially responded negatively toward OSS. They were familiar with and satisfied with the proprietary solutions. A small group of about fifty people, however, welcomed the introduction of OSS, seeing it as an opportunity to learn new applications and acquire new skills.

At sites where training was conducted properly, the level of acceptance of OpenOffice increased quite rapidly. In other cases, however, such as where the training was inadequate or the local IT management did not support OSS, employees initially refused to use the new applications because they considered the migration to OSS to be unnecessary and intrusive. In such cases, the local IT management perceived the migration to be an attack on their independence from the SGV IT department.

As OSS became more widely used, employee attitudes changed. The overall satisfaction rate with OSS rose steadily and, by the end of 2005, about 28% of all documents in the organizations were produced in the OpenOffice format.

At the same time, the employees realized that OpenOffice could both open and use Microsoft Office documents and also support various open data standards. Employees understood that OpenOffice allowed them to work with more data formats. They perceived that OSS was as good as proprietary software in most contexts and, in addition, could guarantee access to old files that the newer versions of proprietary software applications could no longer access.

These factors gradually changed employees' attitudes, beginning with the IT managers. By the beginning of 2006, almost all of the municipalities were involved in the migration process.

Facilitating Conditions

Innovation Attributes
This section discusses some of the attributes of innovation introduced by Rogers (Rogers 2003) and their manifestations at SGV.

Image
The municipalities had IT services that were previously more autonomous and less reliant upon SGV services and perceived the adoption of OSS to involve a loss of independence. Local technicians with limited knowledge of OSS perceived the migration to involve a loss of skills. Moreover, because the introduction of OpenOffice impacted the work of all of the employees of the municipalities, the migration was initially considered to be intrusive and a potential threat to the independence of municipalities as a whole, not just the local IT departments.

This resistance on the part of the municipalities was addressed through mentoring activities and on-site training designed to develop skills and improve user satisfaction. The IT management of SGV publicly disseminated the results and promoted the economic benefits of OSS in order to elicit a positive reaction on a political level, which helped them to inform and persuade the local management of these municipalities.

Relative Advantage

As noted above, SGV's first pilot project failed to communicate the advantages of OSS, which led to problems that users came to associate with OSS.

As a consequence, and because there was no pressure to migrate to OSS for financial reasons, some municipalities delayed the adoption process for several months. During this time, SGV introduced on-site training, developed a tool to convert data standards, and held several meetings with the local managers of the municipalities. These activities sought to promote the advantages of OSS with respect to proprietary software in the minds of the end users. For example, the increased overall knowledge of basic word-processing features and functionalities gave the employees more confidence regarding their IT skills, and small municipalities could develop local competencies for solving general problems involving customization and formatting.

The advantage of being able to open old inaccessible files with OpenOffice was another important point that convinced the managers of municipalities to adopt the new application. It is a fact that newer versions of proprietary software applications generally do not guarantee access to files written with older versions of those applications or the ability to modify older files. OpenOffice was able to guarantee this both for files written in OpenOffice and for files written using other proprietary programs.

Compatibility

The introduction of Linux server-side was compatible with the experience of the IT staff that conducted the migration and used the new operating system. Ten members of the staff had positive previous experiences with the Novell products and were very enthusiastic about the new OSS configuration of the back-end servers. Thus, the migration to Linux was welcomed, because it was expected to ease their work.

Observability

SGV made a special effort to provide employees with generic word-processing training at the same time that it adopted OpenOffice. This enhanced employees' understanding of the similarities and differences of OpenOffice in comparison with Microsoft Office. In particular, employees could recognize and differentiate the general characteristics of a word processor from the specific features of the office application needed in their work (e.g., templates). One observable positive side effect of this training was an increase in the IT competence of nonexpert users.

The approach was different for Group-E. The management wanted to make the transition as smooth as possible by reducing observable effects. Specifically, the user interface of Group-E mimicked the appearance, the features, and the services of the older technology so that the end users did not perceive any changes during the migration. This user representation was possible because the IT staff of SGV was able to interact directly with the local company's development team. The difference between the strategies implemented with OpenOffice and Group-E was determined by this fact. It was not possible to interact with the development team of OpenOffice in the same manner, and extensive training had to be implemented in order to make the transition as smooth as possible.

Organizational Attributes

Absorptive Capacity

Good communication between IT personnel and employees enhanced the trainability of the employees at SGV and the municipalities they serve. The consortium announced the OSS initiative before the first software deployment and held a seminar that both promoted OSS in general and identified specific benefits for public administration.

As mentioned above, SGV converted document templates that were used on a daily basis into the OpenOffice format and provided training regarding the wide range of office automation functions in the suite. These actions gave employees extra incentives to choose OSS and generated more awareness of OSS among all of the stakeholders in the project.

CONCLUSIONS

Table 4.3 presents the differences in SGV's deployment process for the three OSS applications.

Managerial intervention is the key issue here. SGV's IT experts started the migration to OSS by installing Linux—a stable operating system—on the consortium's own servers. This server-side exercise was a success. The IT staff acquired experience and confidence in using OSS, while the changeover had little impact on the daily work of employees in the municipalities.

This success was followed by the implementation of Group-E—the open source communication system. In this case, the impact on employees and their work could have been more

Table 4.3
OSS Deployment within SGV

	OpenOffice	Group-E	Linux for server
Managerial intervention			
Mandatory vs. voluntary usage	Usage was mandatory for the municipalities that depend directly on the central IT department of SGV and voluntary for the larger municipalities with local IT departments.	There was no real perception of the change. The interface to the end user did not change, and the user did not perceive the transition from the old to the new email application.	The migration was conducted server-side. The IT staff was supportive and enthusiastic.
Training and support	SGV held several activities to introduce the new software, including a general introduction to word processors.	External training was provided directly by the software supplier to the central IT department. Maintenance is provided by the external supplier.	External consultancy was needed.
Championing OSS	The chief information officer of SGV had championed OSS since the early stages of the migration. He coordinated the participation of SGV in the European project COSPA as a means of convincing the municipalities of the benefits of OpenOffice for desktop applications and participated in interviews with local and national media in order to disseminate information about the SGV experience outside the organization.	There was no real need of championing OSS as the end-user did not perceive the migration to this new software because the interface for the end-user did not change during or after the migration	There was no need of championing OSS as the internal team already had a positive personal experience with another open tool.

Table 4.3
(continued)

	OpenOffice	Group-E	Linux for server
Subjective norms			
User perceptions	Use of OpenOffice was regarded as a loss of independence in larger municipalities.	No adverse attitude was detected, because the new application was perfectly integrated into the existing system and end users perceived little change.	Linux was installed server-side. The IT staff regarded the migration as innovative.
Facilitating conditions: Innovation attributes			
Image	Municipalities that have local IT departments perceived migration to OpenOffice as a loss of independence.	The new communication system was integrated into the existing environment without modifying the user interface. The change was difficult to perceive.	The migration was server-side, and most of the servers are located at SGV. The IT staff had some experience with Novell and started with a positive attitude regarding OSS.
Relative advantage	Problems related to the first version of OpenOffice were overcome with the subsequent versions of the office suite. Some macros and spreadsheet functions are still considered unstable in OpenOffice compared with Microsoft Office products.	The move away from software vendors produced advantages. For example, the OSS model allows in-house enhancements. General maintenance and support are still provided by the software company that supplied the application.	The migration to Linux was seen as a release from the routine of frequent updates and other forms of control by software vendors.

Table 4.3
(continued)

	OpenOffice	Group-E	Linux for server
Trialability	For Office suites, there was little choice. Although OpenOffice was a valid alternative and was trialable, it was the only valid alternative to Microsoft Office in 2004. Thus, the benefits of trialability were less evident.	The communication system was selected through a search for alternative applications. Choosing an OSS product from a local software company meant that support was readily available.	—
Compatibility	—	—	Linux was perceived as compatible with the previous experience maturated with Novell products
Observability	SGV availed itself of the ability to observe the functionalities of OpenOffice to provide employees with training in the generic functions of a word processor.	—	The success of the Linux installations initiated the general deployment of other OSS applications in SGV and its municipalities.

Facilitating conditions: Organizational attributes

	OpenOffice	Group-E	Linux for server
Absorptive capacity	The training strategy helped overcome initial resistance in the majority of the municipalities.	This capacity was very relevant here because the nontechnical employees did not perceive any difference.	Testing Linux added two to three months to the implementation process, but this effort improved the consortium's ability to use the new operating system.

substantial. The management decided, however, to adopt an open source application from a local software company. This supplier offered technical assistance during the migration process and maintenance support afterward. The new product was completely integrated into an existing information system, and its user interface was difficult to distinguish from the old communication system. Nontechnical users did not notice the difference.

The migration to OpenOffice was the most problematic OSS project for SGV because it involved all of the municipalities and all of their employees. The unsuccessful pilot exercise resulted in negative attitudes toward OSS among end users. The adoption of OpenOffice also uncovered problems related to technical autonomy. Large municipalities with local IT departments felt that the open source office suite made them more dependent on SGV. Unlike Linux and Group-E, which run on central servers managed by SGV, the OpenOffice software was installed on the municipalities' computers, and each authority could decide whether, and when, to use it. In order to help overcome the initial resistance, SGV gave a high priority to on-site training and help desk support. In addition, it arranged the migration process so that it would be led by small municipalities that were more amenable toward adopting OpenOffice.

Secondary Adoption and Assimilation Stage
This section discusses the secondary adoption process and the assimilation of OpenOffice from the perspective of the SGV management because office applications are the core software technologies used by the municipalities of the province.

The adoption process and the assimilation stage were assessed in early 2006 by measuring the use of Microsoft Office and OpenOffice. The daily number of files worked and the number of events performed on these files were used as proxies for the usage of the applications, which served as indicators of the degree of assimilation of OpenOffice.

Two applications[7] that record the files worked and the events on files in a PC were installed to collect this data. These applications run in the background and store data on remote servers. The statistics for May 2005 showed that the two applications collected data from 2,020 PCs in 113 different municipalities. The average daily data transfer to the server was 500 MB, while the average number of files opened each day was about 125,000.

The following analysis examines the data collected from 120 servers in June 2005. The analysis reveals that 6 municipalities worked more than 90% of the time using only OpenOffice, and 23 municipalities used OpenOffice more than 50% of the time. These 23 municipalities reported that they had taken that approach because the new application could open and modify old documents in Microsoft's .doc format. Microsoft Office cannot access OpenOffice files. For the same reason, the results that are reported in figure 4.1 might be overestimated given that measuring the use of files with a given suffix does not imply measuring the use of the application with which those files were created. About ninety users were randomly selected from among the municipalities' employees and monitored for about two months in late 2004. Figure 4.1 illustrates the total number of files created or modified daily in the two office formats per user. On average, users worked on five more Microsoft Office files per day.

In order to understand user perceptions of complexity, events on files per day were analyzed. Figures 4.2 and 4.3

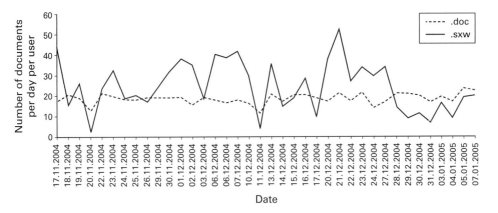

Figure 4.1
Documents created or modified per user per day with the Microsoft
Office (.doc) and Open Office (.sxw) suites.

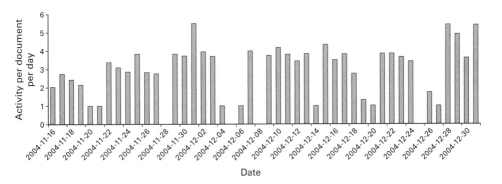

Figure 4.2
Average of events per Microsoft Office document per day.

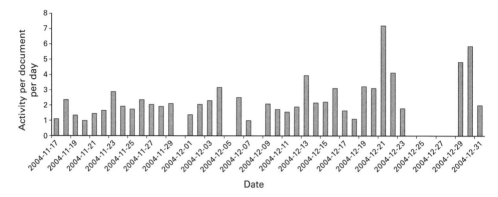

Figure 4.3
Average of events per OpenOffice document per day.

show that this activity differed little between the two applications. On average, a user worked on a Microsoft Office document (3.1 events per file per user) a bit more than was the case for an OpenOffice file (2.6 events per file per user).

This finding was assessed in conjunction with the management strategy favoring OSS adoption and indicates that:

1. The management mandate to use OpenOffice is mitigated by the need to create Microsoft Office files for exchange purposes with external organizations and by the related need to maintain some existing documents in the old format. This factor, together with the incomplete maturity of the migration process, explains the data shown in figure 4.1.

2. The comparable activity on files for the two office suites reveals a similar complexity of use for the two office applications, as shown in figures 4.2 and 4.3.

5
FUNDECYT in Extremadura

INTRODUCTION

The Extremadura region of Spain is the first European case of extensive adoption of OSS in high schools and public offices. Extremadura is one of the poorest regions of Spain. The economy is rural, the population density is quite low, and the urban centers are relatively small. There is a high unemployment rate that has been reported by the national demographic institution Encuesta de Población Activa to be about 23.45%, a rate that is higher than the national average of 20.05% (Eures 2010). The region is outlying and has inadequate transportation and communication infrastructures. Given this background, private companies have never seen the region as a potential market.

Politically speaking, Extremadura is one of the seventeen Spanish autonomous regions with legislative competencies. The region is governed by two major bodies: the Extremadura parliament and the Extremadura regional government (Junta de Extremadura). In the mid-1990s, the regional government decided to invest in developing a global strategy for socioeconomic development that was intended to become a reference point in research and development in information and communication technology (ICT) that would help overcome the outlying character of the region. The vision of the regional government was ambitious (FUNDECYT 2008):

• Accessibility for all; for example, Internet access as a public service

• Stimulation of technological literacy of the population

• Promotion of new enterprises and a new labor culture based on IT.

Given these objectives, a three-pronged strategy was implemented (FUNDECYT 2008):

The actions carried out to reach these objectives have taken place at three different levels: firstly on the Regional Administration (hard and software, training of personnel), secondly in the production sector (aid for companies to adopt new technologies), and thirdly for private users (by offering a diverse selection of mechanisms and tools).

The first action of the government was to establish the Fundación para el Desarrollo de la Ciencia y Tecnología en Extremadura (FUNDECYT) to promote technology and innovation in the Extremadura region. FUNDECYT was established to create synergy between the local university, public administration, and local industry (FUNDECYT 2008):

FUNDECYT has collaborated very actively, together with the Regional Government of Extremadura and other regional bodies, in the implementation of Regional Innovation Strategies (RIS and RITTS) and is currently undertaking the Regional Innovative Actions Programme funded by DG Regio. Under this programme, Extremadura was awarded with the European Prize for its Strategy on ICT.

In particular, the regional strategy in ICT was designed to align the strategic framework with the technological one. The strategy was developed horizontally in order to reach all of the productive and educational areas of the region (figure 5.1).

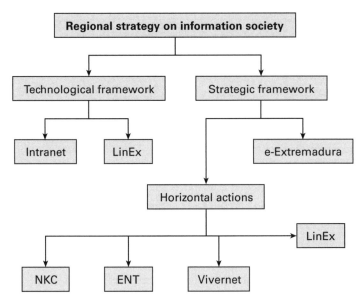

Figure 5.1
The Extremadura regional strategy toward innovation for citizens.
Source: IDABC 2007.

The intranet program was defined to create the connectivity network that would link the major public services at more than 1,400 dispersed sites in the region, such as public offices, schools, and health centers. In 2001, the infrastructure for intranets became available, and the e-Extremadura was established to coordinate European actions regarding innovation in Extremadura. These actions included projects cofounded to increase IT culture in the region, such as thirty-two new knowledge centers (NKCs), the technical education network (ENT) that disseminates scholarly e-content and IT culture in the schools, and a business incubator (Vivernet).

The transition to OSS was one part of this large, ambitious program that involved a cultural change and improvement of regional business activities. It began in 1998 with a preliminary study of the educational software alternatives that were available to the schools. The first major issue concerned the school personnel's limited knowledge of technical English terminology. As a result, the regional government decided to begin a pilot project that included the introduction of a Spanish-language version of Linux that was known as Linux Extremadura (LinEx) (<http://www.linex.org/joomlaex>) in the local schools. The pilot project involved fourteen schools that continued their regular activities during the migration to LinEx. This pilot project was later extended to all of the schools in the province and to regional public administrations. The schools in the region have been using a customized version of LinEx since 2002.

In March 2003, the Andalusia and Extremadura regional governments agreed to cooperate in the distribution of OSS, specifically LinEx. This collaboration included the definition of a common software package to be used in the two Linux distributions that were implemented in Extremadura and Andalusia: LinEx and Guadalinex. LinEx was also installed in other public offices such as the Spanish health-care system. By 2007, LinEx was installed in more than 90,000 PCs in the regional offices.

OSS IN EXTREMADURA

LinEx Project
The LinEx project is a Linux distribution plan that was created to provide citizens with access to local IT services. It is based on Debian, which uses GNOME as its desktop. LinEx

is not inherently innovative; it customizes the generic Linux distribution for purposes of meeting cultural and language localization needs and is specifically designed for use in regional administration and schools. LinEx contains a large amount of software, including the Linux operating systems and several office applications.

LinEx has gone through several major versions since its public launch in 2002. The major turning point came with the gnuLinEx 2003 version. This new version of GNU/LinEx was released and developed by the FUNDECYT development team. Starting with this version, only software released under a GNU general public license (GPL) or GPL-compatible license would be included in the distribution. In early 2009, FUNDECYT launched a new LinEx distribution, which is known as gnuLinEx Lenix (<http://mate.linex.org/linex>). As of 2010, there are several versions that can operate in different environments: LinEx Colegios in the educational system, SESLinEx in the health system, LinEx SP for desktop computers in public offices, LinEx Local for city councils, LinEx PYME for the enterprise sector, juegaLinEx for young people and hobbyists, and gnuLinEx for citizens in general.

The primary role of FUNDECYT was experimentation and encouraging the adoption of LinEx.

The initial deployment and integration of LinEx in schools was outsourced to a national software company. In 2003, the Spanish distribution was managed, maintained, and improved internally by FUNDECYT.

The adoption of LinEx did not generate costs related to data conversion, interfacing with legacy software, and similar typical migration problems because, in the majority of cases, there was no previous software, technology, or infrastructure in place. In the few cases software was already in use, the local

Spanish company provided the necessary upgrades. Most of the costs were incurred in the form of hardware and graphic design. PCs, cables, switches, and other material were needed to create the regional network and to provide schools and public offices with a basic IT infrastructure. Graphic design costs came in the form of Web pages and portals that needed to be designed for use with the new online services.

ANALYSIS OF OSS ADOPTION IN EXTREMADURA

This section illustrates the characteristics of LinEx adoption in Extremadura according to the framework outlined in chapter 2.

Managerial Intervention

Mandatory versus Voluntary Usage
As noted above, the Extremadura regional government had been pushing for the adoption of OSS at the political level since 1998 to reduce public expenditure and to make innovation transparent. The decision to establish an independent organization, FUNDECYT, whose sole mission was to introduce OSS into public administrations, was indicative of the mandatory usage message transmitted by political management to public servants. One consequence was that some resistance to the introduction of the new software arose among employees such as school directors, secretaries, and professors, who, together with the IT staff, had been the primary users of the old proprietary software. Their resistance was founded on several concerns. At the advent of the project, school employees were not properly trained. This occurred because even the IT staff

members in these schools—who were typically senior technicians—were not accustomed to new software platforms. The experience of the parties who were involved had been with proprietary software both for operating systems and office applications. In addition, employees were not accustomed to changing their habits. More particularly, they did not see the benefits to be gained from the introduction of a new software tool, which they considered to be ancillary to their daily educational work.

In order to reduce this resistance, the management of FUNDECYT adopted a threefold strategy: (1) produce a Linux distribution in Spanish based on local needs, (2) outsource the first deployment and integration to a local company, and (3) establish a set of training sessions for all of the end users. In addition, the FUNDECYT management supported the adoption of OSS and led by example by using LinEx itself, which demonstrated an acquired ability to use the new system.

Training and Support

Extremadura conducted a feasibility study and decided to move to a Linux distribution starting with a pilot project to avoid technical problems due to the internal IT staff's lack of experience. This pilot project was outsourced to an external company in Madrid. The Spanish consultant took the existing Linux distribution and customized it to mesh with the language and the needs of the schools.

Part of the first phase of the project was also dedicated to the evaluation of different OSS alternatives for schools. During this stage, five people were hired. After three years, two of them were dedicated to searching for appropriate Linux documentation.

In the meantime, the IT personnel were trained for one year using self-guided learning, and courses and seminars held by the external company.

Although external consultancy was necessary for providing initial training on LinEx and for the subsequent steps taken to help the people become operational with the new platform, the self-guided learning of the IT staff members—which was conducted in their homes in the evening after they attended courses or seminars—was the crucial activity that sped up the learning process. The decisive change in attitude of school personnel could be ascertained by their decision to hire expert Linux operating system technicians.

Championing OSS

In 2003, when the LinEx project was largely diffused, the managing director of Extremadura commented on the project's success:

LinEx is a success due to an administrative and political decision to migrate in a concrete area (education), providing users with the technical support to migrate (including training). Likewise, FLOSS in general is successful if there is a concrete problem (not necessarily a small one) to solve and where proprietary software cannot provide a sustainable solution.

The success of the Extremadura case led to a series of OSS events and studies in public administrations across Europe. This case has been used to demonstrate the viability of OSS in public offices. It became "the example to export," and it was used to champion OSS in the public sector across Europe.

In the case of Extremadura, OSS was more of a necessity than an ideological choice, but, in any case, it resulted in the championing of OSS. The success and promotion of

OSS improved the motivation of employees in the region and became a catalyst and export of OSS culture that was later adopted across Europe and in European public offices.

Subjective Norms

Prior to the OSS migration, the Extremadura region was considered to be a technologically backward area. The OSS migration gave this region an opportunity to improve its reputation for innovation both in Spain and in Europe. In the case of Extremadura, subjective norms were not an individual perception but were rather regional and political in nature. The exposure of Extremadura to OSS increased its technological assets and elevated it to the degree that it became more respected in Europe. This had the side effect of improving the motivation and morale of Extremadura employees, who now perceived that the case could serve as an example that Europe could follow.

Facilitating Conditions

Innovation Attributes

Relative Advantage

The extent to which OSS has been an advantage is incalculable. Prior to the LinEx project, the population of Extremadura had little technological experience or knowledge. Thus, one might speculate that any affordable technology would have enjoyed the same success as OSS experienced. The point is that OSS was the most affordable software technology available at the time. Furthermore, the population of this region naturally perceived OSS as *the* technology of choice and adoption, given that all of the services in the region were equipped with the same technology.

Image

Image was the major issue that concerned teachers and administrative staff in the regional schools. In the initial stage, school personnel were not ready to learn and use the new platform. One reason for this reluctance was that very few people had any prior experience using PCs. Moreover, those people who had such knowledge were accustomed to working on proprietary operating systems (Microsoft Windows 95/98) and proprietary office suites (Microsoft Office). Even the IT staff in the schools—typically one or two not very young technicians—were not quick to adopt the new operating system. Overall, employees of schools were not ready to change their habits, because change suggested additional work or some degree of loss of their power and image.

In order to relieve personnel from the burden of a technological and cultural change, new IT experts were hired. Each school hired a new system administrator who was in charge of maintaining LinEx. It was the role of these administrators to help colleagues learn the basics through a set of training activities. However, there was reluctance and resistance on the part of senior technicians in the schools. They felt a loss of image and deliberately slowed down the rate at which they learned LinEx in spite of the new colleague/trainer assigned to collaborate with them.

The establishment of FUNDECYT contributed to restoring the professional image of the school personnel. It was seen as a concrete long-term project, and the dedicated help of the central government sought to align personnel competencies with modern technologies.

Observability

One of the major positive effects of using OSS was the increase in communication, both internally and externally. This was primarily due to the open access to communities, documentation, and source code that is part of OSS development and adoption. Communication originated from the transparency or observability of OSS.

Internally   The introduction of Linux led to intense discussions among the IT staff members of FUNDECYT and local technicians in the schools. The topics discussed included problem solutions and technical procedures for using specific features of the operating system. In addition, communication between the administrative staff and the IT personnel increased, which helped to resolve technical issues and enhanced the understanding of customization requests.

Externally   The fact that it is possible to access and share experiences with open source communities helped the IT department of FUNDECYT enhance its technical knowledge and to disseminate information about the experience. The IT staff improved its communication with peer bodies in other public administrations in Europe, which allowed the staff to share experiences and ask questions.

Organizational Attributes

General Attitude to Risk

The Extremadura government's decision to provide regional public offices and schools with an open source platform was a risky decision, though it turned out well enough in the end. However, the serious potential risks included the lack of knowledge regarding the feasibility of a migration to OSS, the lack of prior extensive migration, the lack of adoption guidelines, and the limited degree of in-house expertise with OSS. On the other hand, the lack of a budget for IT, the absence of an IT infrastructure that was already in place, and the need to attract industries posed a challenge that needed to be addressed. The government of Extremadura considered sustainability and technological dependency major risks and thus approached OSS adoption as the lesser of two evils. The argument was that any projects that involved informatizing the region would carry unique risks. The government considered the technology and the policy of technological sustainability to be critical to the success or failure of the project. In particular, sustainability was thought of in economic and technological terms: the former in terms of licenses and costs for upgrades and the latter in terms of the employment of internal and external resources required to maintain functional software platforms.

The risk was mitigated by the opportunity to provide a localized version of Linux that had been customized for the Spanish culture. This was fundamental in making the new software acceptable for adoption by nonexpert users, given the population's adverse attitude regarding the use of foreign languages.

Absorptive Capacity
The primary value of OSS in the Extremadura case study was that it provided an IT infrastructure in a context where almost nothing had been in place before. The government of Extremadura recognized the need to create a technological infrastructure and culture before any sort of migration to OSS was carried out. The costs of the hardware and the human

resources were planned and organized to allow regional public offices to absorb the impact of new software technology.

Various activities were conducted that sought to increase the absorptive capacity of the local population. The region was equipped with cable networks and PCs in all of the regional public offices. FUNDECYT was created to help the migration and maintain IT literacy in the region. New technicians were hired in schools. Intensive training, conducted through the consulting company and through FUNDECYT, was provided to all users in order to increase their knowledge of IT and to maintain the productivity of public offices.

Extremadura is currently exporting its adoption model and its platform beyond the region.

Secondary Adoption Process and Assimilation Stage

Prior to the adoption of LinEx, only school directors, secretaries, and professors used PCs, and there were few PCs in use. The most common proprietary office applications were being used. Neither knowledge nor interest in OSS was reported. Following the migration, proprietary and in-house tools were rarely used. Employees and students of the schools who were asked to use LinEx improved their confidence with the platform and went on to become eager to use OSS. The primary reason for this change in attitude stemmed from the friendly interface and the availability of the software product for home use. More specifically, the LinEx interface was customized for use with the Spanish language and culture. For example, office applications were renamed using labels that are common in Spanish culture—for example, the word processor was named Espronceda, which refers to a Spanish writer who lived during the nineteenth century. In addition, students and employees could have LinEx installed on their personal computers at home. This allowed them to use the same applications at home that they used at work or school, which accelerated their learning curves for the new platform.

As noted above, the government's strategy extended to other areas of technological development. The horizontal strategy of the local government accelerated the effective adoption and assimilation of OSS. In 2005, the degree of OSS assimilation reached the general deployment level, that is, the organization made use of the OSS product for at least one large mission-critical system (figure 5.2).

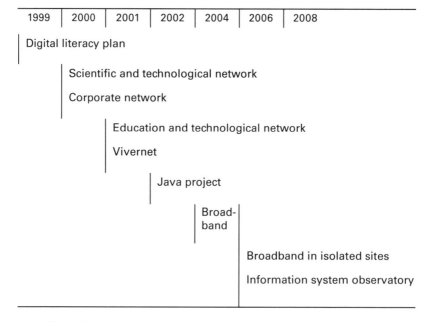

Figure 5.2
Major events and their durations during the implementation plan for research and development and ICT development.

In 2007, the regional government conducted a survey of the population for the purpose of assessing the population's knowledge of LinEx. The results indicated that 42% of the population was familiar with it, and 47% of those who were familiar with confirmed that they used it.

In 2007, 70,000 school computers used LinEx. More than 90,000 users of NKCs, and about 11% of the entire population of Extremadura, confirmed making regular use of NKC services.

CONCLUSIONS

Table 5.1 summarizes the major issues related to the adoption of OSS in Extremadura in light of the framework discussed in chapter 2.

Table 5.1
OSS Deployment within Extremadura

	LinEx in its various versions
Managerial intervention	
Mandatory vs. voluntary usage	The decision to deploy OSS was made by the regional government that funded a pilot project. In particular, the school staff perceived it as mandatory.
Training and support	The regional government defined a well-structured and planned training and support program. An independent public organization, FUNDECYT, was created to support the deployment and assimilation of OSS in all public offices.
Championing OSS	Extremadura became the first reference point for any European public administration that wanted to migrate to OSS. This had a positive effect on the motivation of the local population.
Subjective norms	
User perceptions	Extremadura's exposure to OSS increased its technological assets and improved its position in Europe.
Facilitating conditions: Innovation attributes	
Relative advantage	OSS was *the* technology. It was the most affordable, the most used, and the technology that connected people and services.

Table 5.1
(continued)

	LinEx in its various versions
Image	The establishment of FUNDECYT contributed to restoring the professional image of the school personnel. It was seen as a concrete long-term dedicated form of assistance provided by the central government that sought to align personnel competencies with modern technologies.
Observability	One of the primary positive effects of using OSS was the increase in communication. This was primarily due to open access to communities, documentation, and source code. Communication originated with the observability of OSS.
Facilitating conditions: Organizational attributes	
General attitude to risk	There was no budget for IT, no IT infrastructure in place, and a need to attract industries, which represented a challenge and mitigated the risks associated with adopting OSS.
Absorptive capacity	The primary value of OSS in the Extremadura case study was providing an IT infrastructure where almost nothing had existed before. Various activities were conducted to enhance the absorptive capacity of the local population. Extremadura currently exports its adoption model and LinEx outside the region.

6

Adoption of Open Standards in Massachusetts

INTRODUCTION[1]

In 2003, the Commonwealth of Massachusetts launched a series of new initiatives that sought to foster the use of open standards and OSS. The centerpiece was an open standards policy that required all government-owned IT software to rely on open standards. As a result, Massachusetts became the first U.S. state to adopt an open standards policy. In 2005, this policy was extended to include document formats, and Massachusetts became the first government to mandate the use of the open document format for office applications (ODF). This mandate incorporated de facto use of OpenOffice, an OSS, because it was the only implementation of ODF available at that time.

This chapter relates the history of the open standards policy with respect to the OSS adoption process model and describes the issues concerning the adoption of an open standard policy by applying the framework derived in chapter 2. The resulting analysis shows the utility of the framework for understanding the adoption of the open standards policy.

There are differences between open standards and open source. The definition of *open standards* has never been absolute, and several scholars regard it as a gray area (Krechmer 2006; West 2007). Massachusetts defined an open standard in its policy initiative (I. T. D. Commonwealth of Massachusetts 2004b):

> For the purpose of this policy, open standards are defined as follows: specifications for systems that are publicly available and are developed by an open community and affirmed by a standards body. Hypertext Markup Language (HTML) is an example of an open standard. Open standards imply that multiple vendors can compete directly based on the features and performance of their products. It also implies that the existing information technology solution is portable and that it can be removed and replaced with that of another vendor with minimal effort and without major interruption.

Open standards are specifications for developing software, but OSS is also an approach for developing software. OSS is based on the idea of making the source code for software publicly available. OSS typically relies upon and makes use of open standards. Proprietary software is an alternative development model for OSS, but even proprietary software can utilize open standards. In sum, an open standards policy should not affect the choice of a particular vendor because both open source and proprietary software development models can support open standards.

A number of governments and organizations, including the United States (Committee for Economic Development 2006), the United Kingdom (Office of Government Commerce 2004), Belgium, Finland, France, Japan, Norway, Malaysia, South Africa, and Russia, have called for policies that strongly encourage or mandate the implementation or further evaluation of open standards. Massachusetts is a pioneer in adopting an open standards policy.

This chapter applies the adoption framework to an open standards policy. In general, open standard policies are closely linked to decisions regarding OSS. Once an open standard exists, it is possible for OSS solutions to compete with proprietary ones. Without an open standard, there is no way to ensure that an OSS solution can always compete with proprietary solutions. When Massachusetts initially mandated ODF, it appears to have understood that it would involve migrating from Microsoft Office and to an OSS office suite.

The chapter begins with a short history of the open standards policy in Massachusetts and includes an emphasis on the open formats policy. This discussion relies on the history and analysis of the Massachusetts open standards policy as analyzed in a previous article (Shah, Kesan, and Kennis 2008). In addition, Andrew Updegrove detailed the history of the standards policy in his e-book (Updegrove 2008). The remaining sections discuss the adoption process using the framework derived in chapter 2.

HISTORY OF THE OPEN FORMATS POLICY

In 2002, Jim Willis, who was then the director of e-government for the secretary of state in Rhode Island, pushed the implementation of OSS within the state government (Vaas 2003). Willis was a pioneer—many state governments felt at that time that OSS was not ready for use at the enterprise level. Willis demonstrated that OSS was enterprise-worthy and much less expensive than proprietary software. One year later, Oregon considered a bill that would have required the state to consider using OSS when buying new programs. Although the bill did not give preferential treatment to OSS, it was defeated before a committee vote took place (Bowman 2003; Peterson 2004). Massachusetts took a different approach than the other states with respect to OSS and navigating the associated political trenches.

At first, Massachusetts appeared to follow the lead of Rhode Island and Oregon in not going beyond considering the use of open standards and OSS. Massachusetts—as well as other state governments that create, manage, and store voluminous electronic records—was constrained by IT compatibility, costs, and capability. In September 2003, Eric Kriss, then-secretary of administration and finance in Massachusetts, released a memo to the state's Information Technology Division (ITD) Director Peter Quinn, which stated (Senate Committee on Post Audit and Oversight, Commonwealth of Massachusetts 2006):

[W]e can no longer afford a disjointed and proprietary approach that locks in legacy systems, generates excessive use of outside consultants, and creates long, often misguided project plans. . . . Effective immediately, we will adopt, under the guidance of the Commonwealth's Chief Information Officer Peter Quinn, a comprehensive Open Standards, Open Source policy for all future IT investments and operating expenditures.

On January 13, 2004, the ITD followed up with three separate policy statements concerning open standards and open source. The first policy was an enterprise open standards policy that stated that Massachusetts was moving to open standards for its IT investments (Commonwealth of Massachusetts ITD 2004a). The motives for the new policy were clearly spelled out and included a threefold rationale: government services are delivered more efficiently with system integration and effective data sharing; IT investments should be based on total ownership costs that can be constructed once and used many times by different groups and agencies; and, lastly, open standards are cheaper to acquire, develop, and maintain and do not result in vendor lock-ins.

The second policy was an acquisition policy for all future selections of IT products and services (Commonwealth of Massachusetts ITD 2004a). It mandated "that information technology solutions are selected based on best value after careful consideration of all possible alternatives including proprietary, public sector code sharing and open source solutions." This policy ensured that OSS could be used by the state.

The final policy was an enterprise technical reference manual, which provided a framework for the standards, specifications, and technologies that must be incorporated into prospective IT investments (Commonwealth of Massachusetts 2008). It continues to function as a living document and is updated periodically as the policy evolves. The enterprise technical reference manual is now at version 5.0 and represents a diverse set of technological domains. Twenty-seven technology areas currently fall under its management. The remainder of this section focuses on the issues concerning the policy regarding document formats.

Document formats allow a computer to store memos or spreadsheets. Some well-known document formats are Microsoft's .doc format for word processing, .xls format for spreadsheets, and .ppt format for presentations. Massachusetts sought to move away from Microsoft's proprietary formats and toward open standard document formats. Massachusetts shifted to open standards because it believed that it could lower costs and increase flexibility. These advantages were significant for Massachusetts because they feared that a proprietary standard locked to a proprietary application might result in documents that could become unreadable in five, ten, or one hundred years. Given the rapid development and turnover of software, older proprietary software is often replaced. By using an open standard, Massachusetts believed that it could ensure that documents would be permanently readable.

On September 21, 2005, Massachusetts published version 3.5 of its enterprise technical reference manual, which required that all new documents saved after January 1, 2007 meet the open format guidelines. The notion of open format was redefined to refer to two formats: *open formats*, which include .txt, .rtf, HTML and ODF formats, and *acceptable formats*, which includes the pdf format. Microsoft's document formats were excluded. This policy change would eventually prohibit the use of the default document formats found in Microsoft Word, Excel, and PowerPoint and other proprietary document formats used by other vendors. This exclusion was important and drew immediate attention to the Massachusetts policy.

Among the acceptable open formats listed was ODF, a standard that began as an XML interchangeable file format for Sun's StarOffice product. It was initially used in StarOffice and OpenOffice, the latter being a freely available office suite program. The adoption of ODF as an open standard for office applications was made under the aegis of an industry consortium known as the Organization for the Advancement of Structured Information Standards (OASIS).

Microsoft responded to its exclusion and the concerns that had been raised by Massachusetts. It began by opening up its new XML document formats, which are the successors to the current document formats (e.g., .doc format) and which eventually became known as Office Open XML (OOXML). It submitted OOXML to two international standards bodies, the European-based Ecma International and the ISO. Microsoft also posted a "covenant not to sue" regarding its Office XML formats, thus easing the licensing requirements. The covenant was founded upon Microsoft's earlier agreement regarding royalty-free licensing.

While Microsoft was responding to Massachusetts's criticism, a new form of opposition to the document formats policy emerged. Beginning in March 2006, disability advocates publicly voiced strong concerns over the planned switch from Microsoft Office to an ODF-compliant OSS office suite such as OpenOffice. Disabled workers depend on extra technologies that are usually developed by third-party vendors who primarily catered to Microsoft products due to their domination of the document-creation market (Noyes 2006). The advocates for the disabled argued that without Microsoft they would lose accessibility.

A Massachusetts state senate committee, chaired by Senator Marc Pacheco, released a blistering report in June 2006, which criticized the open standards measure (Senate Committee on Post Audit and Oversight, Commonwealth of Massachusetts 2006). The report argued that the policy had been drafted and implemented in an undemocratic, closed-room manner and recommended delaying the plan's 2007 implementation unless the ITD acceded to a number of measures, including demonstrating its accessibility for disabled state workers.

Despite the public relations damage inflicted by the report and opposition by disability advocates, then-Governor Mitt

Romney maintained his support for the plan, and the ITD did not delay its implementation. However, in order to address the concerns raised about accessibility, the ITD had to change its implementation strategy in order to accommodate Microsoft Office products. This required a plug-in for Microsoft Office to support ODF and delayed the implementation process. The deadline was extended to June 2007. Even with this extension, as of late June 2007, only 250 of the state's computers had been successfully equipped with software plug-ins that enabled conversion abilities (create, read, and save) for the change to ODF (Lai 2007b).

On August 1, 2007, version 4.0 of the enterprise technical reference manual officially added Microsoft's OOXML to the approved list of open formats (Pepoli and Dormitzer 2007). In revising the enterprise technical reference manual, Massachusetts recognized that Microsoft had made several changes to OOXML, including moving OOXML to a standards organization, adding a covenant not to sue, and getting it approved as an open standard by Ecma International in 2006. Massachusetts officially reasoned that, "there is industry support for Open XML and we believe that by adopting the standard we will be able to accelerate the pace of migration to XML document formats" (Lai 2007a).

Despite the painstaking evolution of the enterprise technical reference manual and Microsoft's efforts to adhere to Massachusetts's criteria for open standards, as of January 2008, both OOXML and ODF were little-used by the government of Massachusetts. A Google search identified 17,300 .doc files, 31 .odt files based on ODF, and 0 .docx files based on OOXML. These numbers include only files that are publicly available through the Web site for the Commonwealth of Massachusetts (<http://www.mass.gov>) but suggest how infrequently these standards are used. Nevertheless, the latest office suites, such as Microsoft Office and OpenOffice, all make use of ODF or OOXML, so the numbers of files are likely to rise as users begin using these new formats.

Several other states have considered legislation that would mandate open standards for document formats. OOXML was only recently approved as meeting ISO standards, and these bills effectively encouraged or mandated the ODF format. To date, open format initiatives have failed in many states, including Connecticut, Florida, Texas, Oregon, California, and Minnesota. These failures can be explained by the fear of the implementation problems that arose with ODF and an initial lack of cost savings, which made the transition to ODF too problematic to undertake. As a result, states are beginning to move in a slower, more measured manner. In New York, a recent bill resulted in a study of how government can incorporate open formats (New York State Chief Information Officer 2008). While it is true that states understand the benefits of open standards, they are currently taking a more cautious approach to open formats and are seeking a clearly specified set of benefits.

ANALYSIS OF OPEN STANDARDS ADOPTION

This section discusses the adoption of the open standards policy using the framework derived in chapter 2.

Managerial Intervention
The open standards policy persisted due to a strong organizational commitment for the policy, despite occasional criticism.

The Massachusetts open formats policy broke new ground. Massachusetts was the first government in the world to mandate ODF. Initiating and maintaining such a policy required resources, knowledge, and commitment. The state government faced considerable criticism for its decision from the Massachusetts Software Council, the legislature, and advocacy groups.

This policy lasted for several years due to the commitment of a number of key public officials: Information Technology Division's (ITD) CIO Peter Quinn and Director Louis Gutierrez, Secretary Eric Kriss, and Governor Mitt Romney. These officials understood the relevant issues and trusted the technical judgment of the ITD and its implementation plan. Without their strong organizational commitment, the standards policy initiative would have collapsed. Their support helped pressure Microsoft to change its licensing policy, move its OOXML document format into a standards body, and support ODF plug-in technologies.

A central part of the adoption framework is managerial intervention. In this case, without the leadership and the knowledgeable and committed support, Massachusetts would not have decided to transition to open formats and would not have sustained its policy for four years while attempting to implement a pioneering policy. This managerial leadership was a key difference between Massachusetts and other states that considered, but did not implement, such a policy.

Subjective Norms
Subjective norms concern how individuals believe their peers and coworkers expect them to behave in relation to technology. From the values and norms perspective, the ideology

represented by OSS can influence the adoption process. In the case of Massachusetts, the ideological values of OSS were constrained by the importance of making reasoned and pragmatic government decisions.

The subjective norms in the adoption process were dominated by concerns regarding pragmatism and saving money for the citizens of Massachusetts. For example, Peter Quinn, the former CIO, refers to the decision making as being "driven by the business of best value and good government" (Quinn 2006). In a similar manner, the guidance for the standards strategy suggested that standard strategy "rationalizes IT investments, reduces risk, finds best ways to extend IT, and promotes flexibility and interoperability" (Massachusetts Information Technology Commission 2003). These norms show how little influence there was over the subjective norms of OSS.

Facilitating Conditions

Chapter 2 discussed several innovation attributes that previous research has determined influences innovation adoption. This section discusses the attributes that are most relevant to the open standards policy—relative advantage, compatibility, complexity, and trialability.

Innovation Attributes

Relative Advantage

The open standards policy was seen as offering two distinct relative advantages in Massachusetts. These advantages constitute part of the reason why the policy was initiated and sustained.

First, the policy appeared to have the potential to produce significant economic savings. Massachusetts saw open standards as having the potential to reduce costs not only through competition but also through a reduction in total ownership costs. The ITD said that open standards are a "more cost-effective 'build once, use many times' approach" (Commonwealth of Massachusetts ITD 2004b). The central idea was that once a standard is put into use and implemented, it can then be used many times by different groups and agencies.

Massachusetts believed that a move to ODF could save money. The ITD conducted a back-of-the-envelope financial analysis and determined that switching to ODF and adopting OpenOffice would cost about $8 million. OpenOffice was a freely available implementation of ODF at that time. In contrast, remaining with Microsoft Office and paying for Microsoft's Office 12 would result in costs of $34 million. ITD thus thought that it could save the state $26 million by using ODF and OSS (Senate Committee on Post Audit and Oversight, Commonwealth of Massachusetts 2006). These figures were later called into question and shown to be erroneous. However, at the time, ITD believed that it was saving money.

Second, the use of open standards for document formats offered Massachusetts freedom from being locked into proprietary formats. This allowed it to ensure that the history of its documents would be available to all. No party could control access to public records.

At the outset of Massachusetts's announcement of the new open standards policy, it was made clear that the greatest incentive for the change was avoiding vendor lock-in (Commonwealth of Massachusetts ITD 2004b). Vendor lock-in occurs whenever customers' buying choices are tied to their prior purchases of related products. Consumers of IT products are particularly susceptible to vendor lock-ins. The significant cost of switching is the essential component that determines vendor lock-ins, which prevents the realization of user choice and flexibility (Marks 2004).

Massachusetts ITD officials hoped that putting an open standards measure into place in relation to document formats would limit vendor lock-ins. Eric Kriss, the Massachusetts secretary of finance and administration, elucidated this rationale regarding open formats in stark terms (Weisman 2005):

Open formats are at the very heart of our democratic process. The question is whether a sovereign state has the obligation to ensure that its public documents remain forever free and unencumbered by patent, license, or other technical impediments. We say, yes, this is an imperative. Microsoft says they disagree and want the world to use their proprietary formats.

Compatibility
Compatibility was not initially believed to be an issue in the Massachusetts decision. This quickly changed, however, once the ITD realized that it had overlooked an important stakeholder in the process. Compatibility problems slow the adoption of OSS.

The Massachusetts open formats policy suffered a serious setback when it failed to take into consideration the impact of changing software on all of its users (Office of the State Auditor 2006). Before Massachusetts mandated ODF, disabled workers and their representatives voiced their concerns to the ITD. According to the president of the Disability Policy Consortium, John Winske, these concerns met with no response from ITD. This turned out to be a mistake for the ITD. The representatives of disabled workers took their concerns to the press, where they received sympathetic attention. In retrospect, the former CIO of the ITD, Peter Quinn, admitted that this was a key tactical error and that, if he were able to do things over again, he would have handled matters differently and paid more attention to the concerns of the disabled workers. In fact, shortly after the policy was formulated, Quinn went so far as to apologize for having neglected to consult with the representatives of disabled workers at a public hearing held in October 2005 (Gardner 2005).

The core problem was that Microsoft Office supported the accessibility software that was required by some disabled users, while OpenOffice and other OSS office suites did not provide robust accessibility features. Microsoft Office did not support ODF, which forced the ITD to look for a way to make Microsoft Office compatible with ODF. The resulting approach was not well-thought out and technically complex. It required a plug-in to make Microsoft's office suite compatible with the ODF. As a result, compatibility between ODF and Microsoft became a significant problem. Massachusetts missed its timetable for implementing ODF due to the delays that resulted.

Complexity
The complexity issue is related to the compatibility issue. Massachusetts initially believed that the adoption of ODF and the shift from Microsoft Office to OpenOffice would not be very complex. However, once it began the transition, it found that the transition was substantially more complicated than anticipated. For example, during the transition, Massachusetts was forced to switch from using an open source office suite back to Microsoft Office with plug-ins. This switch was

done to accommodate the community of people with disabilities. However, this change also proved problematic, because plug-in solutions did not yet exist and had to be developed. The resulting technical issues were unforeseen and prolonged the process of implementing ODF.

Trialability

During the discussions in Massachusetts regarding OSS adoption, trialability was a benefit Peter Quinn raised. He was a fan of OSS because he liked the idea of being able to share code. He also liked the idea that something could be built once, and everyone could then share it (Quinn 2006). This offered a crucial advantage over proprietary applications, for which sharing code with other states through the negotiation of individual contracts was untenable.

The ITD supported a related trialability project—sharing OSS between governments. This project is known as the Government Open Code Collaborative. Its mission is to encourage sharing, at no cost, computer code developed for and by government entities where the redistribution of this code is allowed.

Organizational Attributes

One important organizational attribute of Massachusetts was the willingness to be first. This characteristic may have influenced its adoption of the open standards policy. The ITD often pointed out that Massachusetts has a long history of being first when it comes to public issues. More specifically, Massachusetts was the first state to create a public library, a public school, and a public subway. Without taking anything away from the strength of the individual leaders within the

Massachusetts government, this commitment to the broad advancement of overarching public policy efforts contributed and made it comfortable for Massachusetts to embrace an open standards policy. That said, some of the initial, broad commitment to the development of open standards was mediated, with the passage of time, by the realities on the ground.

Secondary Adoption Process and Assimilation Stage

Secondary adoption in this case study is mixed. The movement to OSS essentially ended once OOXML was approved. After the approval of OOXML, there was no longer a serious impetus to use OpenOffice. However, there was some limited testing of various types of OSS. The ITD initially tested the use of OpenOffice, and 250 of the state's computers were later successfully equipped with OSS software plug-ins that enabled conversion abilities (create, read, and save) for the change to ODF (Lai 2007b).

CONCLUSIONS

The chapter examined the Massachusetts policy shift toward open standards for document formats using the adoption framework discussed in chapter 2. The adoption framework highlights several crucial issues that affected the adoption of the open standards policy and OSS. A summary of the analysis is provided in table 6.1.

The major factors that initiated, pushed, and maintained the adoption of the standards policy included the managerial leadership, the relative advantages of open standards, and the trialability of OSS. However, during the process,

Table 6.1
Massachusetts's Open Standards Policy

	Open standards policy
Managerial intervention	
	Strong leadership, together with knowledgeable and committed support, allowed the policy to persevere.
Subjective norms	
	The ideological values of OSS were constrained by the importance of making reasoned and pragmatic government decisions.
Facilitating conditions: Innovation attributes	
Relative advantage	First, the policy had the potential to produce significant economic savings. Second, open standards offered Massachusetts more freedom.
Compatibility	Compatibility was initially overlooked but later become a major issue when OpenOffice turned out to be incompatible with software that helps disabled people.
Complexity	Complexity became an issue when the ITD was forced to switch from OpenOffice to a more complex plug-in solution for Microsoft Office.
Trialability	Trialability was seen as an attractive and useful feature of OSS.
Facilitating conditions: Organization attributes	
	There was a history of path-breaking public service projects from an organizational view; this helped the strong state leadership maintain a commitment to open standards.
Secondary adoption process and assimilation stage	
	There was an initial trial of OpenOffice and plug-in solutions.

developments related to compatibility and complexity slowed the adoption process. Finally, other issues, such as subjective norms, organizational attributes, and the secondary adoption process, played secondary roles in the adoption process. In sum, the adoption framework in chapter 2 is a useful analytic approach for understanding the adoption of the Massachusetts open standards policy.

7

The Italian Chamber of Deputies

INTRODUCTION[1]

The Italian Chamber of Deputies (the Chamber), *Camera de deputati* in Italian, is one of the most important parts of the government in Italy. It is one of the two chambers of the Italian parliament. The Italian constitution assigns it legislative power, together with the senate of the republic. Every five years, 630 deputies are elected to the Chamber. Due to its central role in public life, the Chamber has authority over a variety of topics, including agriculture, the economy, culture, and military defense. For this reason, many commissions (generally fourteen, among them foreign affairs, defense, and justice) prepare their work for the general assembly, where decisions and laws are discussed and voted upon. Every act of the Chamber follows a structured workflow that is defined by the Italian constitution and by law. Any action undertaken by the Chamber must be properly supported by a software system that manages the different workflows. This is necessary to help ease the large amount of information that must be published and made available to the public through Web sites and Web services. For instance, it is possible to retrieve all of the available information concerning the work of a specific deputy, in terms of legal proposals, actions, presence in parliament, and so on. In addition, the Chamber has its own Web TV channel that broadcasts the meetings of deputies, as well as institutional communications.

As noted above, the Chamber consists of 630 deputies, each of whom is assisted by a number of staff members. The administration of the Chamber has the mission of supporting the general assembly in all of its activities. For this reason, about 4,000 people are employed by the Chamber, and that number is divided into organizational units that are known as *services*. They maintain and support the established workflows, gather information about topics that are under discussion in the general assembly or by commissions, and interact with the senate and other public administrative bodies, such as the ministries.

The employees of the Chamber are seen as being elite members of the public administration of Italy and rank highly in terms of productivity and efficiency. They are renowned for their commitment and are proud of their reputation. Thus, any initiative that is launched and supported by top management is taken seriously and supported by all employees.

The ICT department consists of about seventy employees whose mission is to support the work of the deputies (630), their staff (about 700) and the administration (about 1,400). The ICT department provides software that helps the deputies and the administration cope with the demanding requirements of their complex organization. The ICT department has externalized certain activities and, in some cases, has acted as a central coordination nexus between pools of companies and has given them direction regarding how to integrate their activities with the other parts of the IT infrastructure in a coherent manner. The heterogeneous activities of the Chamber led to the decision to acquire custom software from publicly selected vendors. However, this has sometimes led to situations in which the maintenance and upgrade costs of deployed solutions tended to increase. In addition, it was nearly impossible to change support partners, due to lock-in strategies that had been put in place over the course of time.

OSS IN THE CHAMBER OF DEPUTIES

In this context of vendor lock-in and growing maintenance costs, the Chamber looked to OSS for a solution. OSS and its increasing standards of performance were informally monitored by the Chamber. Many activities related to OSS had been promoted by the head of the document management office, who provided much of the information that appears in this chapter.

OSS was considered to be much more than simply a technological choice: it was regarded as a strategic consideration. The motivation for considering OSS was to provide the administration with a fine-grained control of the software it uses that would not be subject to commercial or technical constraints imposed by vendors. OSS was adopted as a driver that would limit lock-in attempts that might stem from software vendors in various application contexts, from servers to desktop environments. A number of activities were initiated that sought to deploy customized OSS to cope with the specific requirements of the Chamber.

A list of OSS used in relevant projects includes:

- OpenOffice
- Zimbra collaboration suite
- Alfresco
- Solr and Lucene (for information retrieval).

The possibility of using, adopting, and/or integrating these software packages in different initiatives and the potential for reducing licensing expenses induced the Chamber to budget for software in a new and different manner.

The vendor negotiation process became more transparent because it was founded on defining customization and integration implementation, together with estimated relative costs. Even in the case of dual-licensed software (i.e., software that requires the purchase of a license for commercial use), negotiation focused more on the acquisition of service than on the software license. In this manner, the Chamber was not bound to any specific vendor of any particular software product but only to the actual service. This consideration refocused attention on the commercial negotiations, which generally lowered overall prices.

Moreover, given that the internal dynamics of OSS were more observable (e.g., in terms of the availability of the source code repository and the software development process), it was possible to conduct software inspections. For example, it was possible to inspect software for the purpose of ensuring that a software product maintained appropriate levels of quality and security.

OSS DESKTOP AND OPENOFFICE

OSS has been used in the Chamber for fifteen years, particularly for back-end services, such as firewalls, the Domain

Name System (DNS), and mail servers. The rise of OSS in the Chamber began in 2006, when deputies officially requested that the administration of the Chamber use OSS software in any and all possible contexts. At that point, a committee was established to create an OSS desktop environment that was customized to meet the needs of the Chamber. After evaluating different GNU/Linux desktop distributions available on the market, the final choice was SuSE Linux by Novell, which provided optimized support to OpenOffice. In early 2007, the GNU/Linux distribution for the Chamber was released. However, adoption was difficult because some needs could only be met with software available on Microsoft systems, which is a good example of lock-in. In order to overcome this problem, ICT management decided to postpone migration to the OSS desktop. It instead began to migrate from Microsoft Office to OpenOffice but on Microsoft systems, thus moving the dependent software to the new office productivity solution. The migration process to OpenOffice came to completion at the end of 2010, given that there was an accelerated deployment strategy. By September 2010, a number of internal departments had already managed a successful migration: the ICT, library, administration, and the parliamentary control, which adds up to about 10% of employees of the Chamber. During the migration process, a number of technical obstacles were removed. For example, some departments required Microsoft software to conduct their activities but were able to migrate to OpenOffice. Studies Services had produced a huge set of documents, using customized word-processor services, and those were also migrated to OSS. Most problems were resolved, and it was regarded as a successful migration.

The project was considered groundbreaking both for the results achieved and in terms of project management and the cooperation of public administrators with local industries and research bodies. The primary partners of the project were two Italian small- to medium-sized enterprises and an Italian university (the Free University of Bolzano-Bozen). From the management's perspective, the project was a success, particularly in terms of industrial policy. The involved partners collaborated with customers to produce feasibility studies and implement customization services and other activities. The project represented an opportunity for the Chamber to gather highly skilled resources from the local community and to reacquire competencies and skills for a fundamental technology: the office automation suite.

OSS IN THE STRATEGY OF THE CHAMBER

The results obtained by the OSS project produced a change in the strategic attitude of ICT management. In recent years, projects initiated by ICT management, such as the new intranet portal, have been designed using OSS components exclusively. New projects are now expected to make use of OSS. When this is not the case, it is necessary for the proponents to justify their motivation for excluding existing OSS elements in favor of proprietary software.

Analysis of OSS Adoption in the Italian Chamber of Deputies

This section focuses on the migration toward the GNU/Linux desktop system and OpenOffice within the Chamber using the framework in chapter 2.

Managerial Intervention

Mandatory versus Voluntary Usage

The project had the full support of the top management of the Chamber, which had a positive effect on the morale and acceptance of the project among the deputies. Making the project official by means of a public decision ensured the highest level of commitment that was possible for an initiative within the Chamber. The ICT department estimated that there would be a dramatic decrease in expenses that would bring the license and maintenance budget (after the transition) down to one-seventh of the original expenses. Thus, the users accepted the migration as being unavoidable and the best option to pursue, given the established political tendency to reduce costs in the Italian public administration. Finally, the project was promoted to users by marketing it as a true solution to the problems faced by the administration that made use of a pragmatic approach and that did not involve ideological motivation. The project was instead presented as a natural form of evolution of the IT infrastructure. This did not mean, however, that the process was regarded as involving a worsening of working conditions. On the contrary, the feedback of users to date has been quite positive overall. The primary motivation for this attitude, as indicated to ICT management by users, was the technical effectiveness and adequacy of the solutions considered. OpenOffice users in particular perceived it as being similar to Microsoft Office. This feeling was reinforced during the training phase, which included a motivational session on the project. However, there remain some unresolved issues, such as file format management issues that were reported by users and some difficulties in modifying established daily habits. The managers stated that, after adoption, as increasing numbers of users became involved and guidelines became available, the majority of issues would be resolved, given that the issues primarily involved interactions between users who had already migrated and users who continued to use the old system.

Training and Support
The managers of the migration process did not underestimate the importance of training and support. They designed them in consultation with external consultants who were experienced in OpenOffice migrations and had been hand-picked from industry and academia. The consultants' role consisted of helping the managers design training sessions and produce training materials. They also conducted the early pilot training program for the first set of users.

Target users for the migration of the office automation suite were chosen on the basis of their interest in and ability to use word processors. Their knowledge and comfort level with Microsoft Word was generally acceptable, but they were slightly less comfortable with the other parts of the office automation suite. Given this, the training and support strategy included topics structured "by difference." For example, the training team developed a set of guidelines and translation principles for the most commonly used features so that the Chamber could move from Microsoft Word to OpenOffice easily. In this manner, it became straightforward to learn how to use OpenOffice, which primarily involved memorizing different commands. There was another level to the training materials, which explained the different commands, and this was followed by additional details for advanced users.

Advanced features of the OpenOffice suite were explained step by step. This was done both to prepare the novice OpenOffice users and to encourage application literacy and more specific knowledge of office suites in general. In this manner, the training sessions were an added value for users, because they led some users to discover and learn new features that could be useful in everyday activities.

The training sessions were structured in a manner that combined face-to-face teaching with e-learning services. Each session was structured to involve about four hours of face-to-face teaching, together with a follow-up e-learning suite (Moodle),[2] which allowed users to interact as a community while being assisted by external experts through forums and wikis. The face-to-face sessions were conducted in classes with a maximum of nine users in order to ensure a high-quality level of interaction between users and the two tutors. The first hour was devoted to explaining the motive behind the project, which was followed by three hours of user training on Writer, Calc, and Impress. In cases where particular users had specific needs, the Impress software was explained in greater detail. The tutors alternated between offering explanations and demonstrating hands-on use of the software programs. The final half-hour was dedicated to teaching users how to use an e-learning system. This was done to provide the users with the means to keep in touch with the rest of the community and to continue their discussions and troubleshooting. During the sessions, tutors also provided a set of guidelines that were intended to help users avoid interoperability issues until the migration process was completed.

The tutors were not external to the Chamber. They were users who had originally been trained by external consultants and were selected on the basis of their skills and passion for the project for specific training that would help them train others.

The support process consisted of improving existing help-desk services, training operators to support users in their OpenOffice tasks, and using the online e-learning service as a knowledge base that could be consulted as needed to solve specific problems.

Subjective Norms

Most users embraced the migration in a collaborative and collegial spirit. The users attempted to learn about the new software as quickly as possible so that they could proceed with their work as usual. It appears that users perceived the introduction of OpenOffice to be an unavoidable form of evolution of the workplace that did not have any significant implications for their everyday activities, so they thus felt little reason to resist or complain. It is possible that there was very little upheaval because the new software was being exchanged for a very similar type of software. If there had been a shift in political power within the group or organization, there probably would have been a greater degree of reaction, positive and negative. Moreover, when the project began, the management of the ICT department unexpectedly discovered that a number of users were already using OpenOffice at home or in other contexts. The project management wisely decided to involve these individuals as resources within departments and offices who could be called upon to help their colleagues during the early stages of the migration.

Facilitating Conditions

Innovation Attributes

IMAGE

This project was fortunate in being backed by top management and the administration, who spelled out the benefits that would be achieved by the migration. Moreover, there was a generally positive attitude toward the change, while the lowest level of enthusiasm was neutrality. These reactions, which ranged from ambivalence to enthusiasm, helped to ensure that there was a smooth transition from Microsoft Office 97 to OpenOffice (versions 2.4 and 3.0). The factors mentioned above contributed to the creation of an image that ranged from neutral to positive for OpenOffice. Such a response from the potential users was consistent with the migration strategy, which positioned OpenOffice as being an alternative software program that was little different than Microsoft Office. An interesting example that reveals the positive inclinations of users regarding OpenOffice occurred when a technical problem arose, and a patch was rapidly developed by the support company to fix it. The users who were directly affected by the bug (a small group of users, because the problem affected only Calc) had negative feelings about the software, but they were impressed by the solution that was obtained, which helped to reinforce confidence in the project managers and their choice to migrate to OpenOffice. After the upgrade from OpenOffice 2.4 to 3.0, it was discovered that the locking mechanism that allowed users to work collaboratively on the same spreadsheet file was not included in the newer version. This situation was unacceptable for a department that made substantial use of this feature while concurrently editing a set of spreadsheet files. A patch was developed in less than a week by the service company. After a period of testing, it was distributed to the users. This was a serious problem that worried the users and induced them to question the migration. However, the solution was offered to them so rapidly that they were clearly impressed, and it confirmed that the management and support team were reliable and available in the event of need.

RELATIVE ADVANTAGE, COMPATIBILITY, AND COMPLEXITY

The relative advantage for the users of OpenOffice was closely tied to the specific features with which they were familiar. Another interesting feature that was explicitly mentioned in the guidelines for the migration was the ability to send documents via email using pdf or Microsoft Office formats. This made it easier for users to exchange documents with others in the administration who had yet to migrate and with external recipients. In order to further simplify the process and the interactions of the users during the project, the management commissioned the development of an OpenOffice extension that allowed a selection of documents (one or more) to be sent as attachments by email. The innovation here was that OpenOffice documents could automatically be converted into their respective Microsoft Office formats.

Compatibility between OpenOffice and Microsoft Office was generally perceived to be quite good. However, this result was achieved only after substantial effort and a serious implementation strategy. The implementation strategy involved certain conversion activities for the most frequently used document templates in the department. In this manner, the most common issues were avoided. Management was surprised that users did not complain about increasing complexity as new software was progressively introduced and that they found the guidelines clear. Any difficulties that arose from user experiences were resolved through the training sessions and the just-in-time e-learning services, as was also the case with the forums.

TRIALABILITY

During the last ten years, the ICT department had privileged OSS alternatives. However, the adequacy of such software with respect to the demanding requirements of the Chamber had to be properly demonstrated and verified. Thus, the trialability of candidate software was an important factor that could help support new proposals. In the case of OpenOffice, the process was particularly easy, and ICT management enjoyed the opportunity to test it in real-life contexts before beginning the actual migration process. Moreover, different OpenOffice distributions had been considered, and having had the opportunity to test each of them allowed management to make a sound and workable choice. In the case of the new intranet portal, which was based on OSS, ICT management benefited immensely from being able to evaluate its various components before its final integration into the product. Every component passed a number of evaluations that contributed to the design of a successful integration strategy for the final product. In addition, given the possibility of finding more than one company that could operate as a potential consultant for an OSS product, the trialability of software was available to a variety of external vendors. The fact that they were dealing with OSS implied that potential partners could also experiment with the software. Several vendors had enjoyed the opportunity to present their solutions, customizations, and plans for cooperation on different projects. The level of innovation increased because various versions of OpenOffice had different support companies, all of which could now offer their own customizations. Trialability thus became a relevant element of the managerial strategy of the Chamber for OSS adoption.

Organizational Attributes

ABSORPTIVE CAPACITY

The strong absorptive capacity of the Chamber was a key factor in all of its OSS projects. In the case of OpenOffice, the design of the communication strategy, as well as the choice of the specific training and support system, was explicitly conceived for the purpose of easing adoption and smoothing the implementation process. The feedback of users demonstrated the effectiveness of this strategy, and users accepted the process. Moreover, the ICT department sought to acquire the skills and tools necessary to administer the process from top-level external consultants (who came from both industry and academia), which reduced the technological risks. The outcome of adopting this approach was the acquisition of new competencies with relatively limited effort. This allowed them to become acquainted with not only the specific software in use but also with the principles and guidelines concerning OSS migrations. The benefits in terms of enhancement of skills and competencies in technical and organizational matters allowed this project to be considered as a reference and a form of internal guidance for the Chamber. The intranet portal, in fact, followed the same organizational and technical principles, because no previously existing software had to be replaced. Many alternative OSS products had been deployed and evaluated by the ICT department, which proved that the new OSS environment that had been established did not cause problems for the staff. These considerations supported the notion that the absorptive capacity of the Chamber was strong, given the specific problem-solving skills that had been acquired.

CONCLUSIONS

The OpenOffice project at the Chamber was seen as successful. There was support and commitment from top management, and widespread user acceptance (achieved through the strategic leveraging of training and support) reflected the absorptive capacity.

Trialability played an important role in the design of the migration process, because it allowed for the selection of the particular OpenOffice distribution that was most appropriate for coping with the technical and organizational requirements of the Chamber. This selection process enabled the evaluation of possible technical partners in terms of the levels of support and development of extensions they offered. While trialability helped in the selection of specific solutions, the absorptive capacity of the technical staff permitted the acquisition of new OSS solutions in the existing environment in a straightforward manner and in the same capacity with respect to the users, which enhanced the acceptance of OSS solutions.

Despite some technical problems that arose during the upgrade of OpenOffice from version 2.4 to 3, overall confidence in the project was reinforced by the solutions that were rapidly produced by the ICT department, in cooperation with external consultants, which counterbalanced any negative feelings that might have been created.

To summarize the experience, the holistic strategy adopted by ICT management enjoyed commitment from top management of the Chamber and made use of a focused communication strategy. It was developed through the use of specific training and support phases, and led users to accept the project and adapt to it, even in the face of technical issues (mostly noncritical and seldom obstructing the use of OpenOffice). A summary of the analysis is given in table 7.1.

The above reasons, considered in conjunction with the framework in chapter 2, allow it to be stated that the degree of assimilation by the Chamber for the OSS project promoted a successful general deployment.

Table 7.1
OSS Deployment within the Italian Chamber of Deputies

	OpenOffice
Managerial intervention	
Mandatory vs. voluntary usage	Users perceived the project as being un-avoidable, given the forced cuts in expenses and top-management commitment. They did not exhibit any serious resistance to the project. Differences between OSS and proprietary systems were downplayed. High levels of training were available, and power users were trained to act as promoters in every department.
Training and support	Several activities helped introduce the new software. A half-day training workshop was held to explain the most commonly used features of the software, and an e-learning community was set up.
Subjective norms	
	Users accepted the new software, and no significant difference was reported between the old and new systems.
Innovation attributes	
Image	The perception of the project was slightly positive, because the users shared the migration process objectives.
Relative advantage	Users perceived the new solution as an advantage because it offered certain unique features beyond what the general office automation suite offered.
Trialability	The ICT management made good use of trialability in choosing the OpenOffice distribution to use and indirectly in choosing the support company.
Organization attributes	
Absorptive capacity	The communication and training strategy helped reinforce the absorptive capacity of users, and the ICT management adapted quite well to the new open source environment.

8

Comparing the Case Studies

This book represents the first in-depth analysis of case studies of secondary adoption of OSS in public administrations. Adoption in public organizations is steered by investment policies oriented toward the goal of limiting public spending, while at the same time improving the quality of services delivered to citizens and the interactions between internal personnel and the citizenry. On the other hand, the strategies and policies of public bodies are strongly conditioned by external sociopolitical directives. In this dichotomy, adopting new technologies is a major change and can create an assimilation gap during the adoption process.

In the case of public-sector employees, the implementation of an innovation strategy is addressed to a heterogeneous set of users who might have little interest in the new technology or might even oppose making such a change if it is perceived to impact their preferred manner of working. In the case of the public sector, where little professional advancement may be possible, there are very few reasons for change that will motivate the average employee.

The role of open source in technology adoption remains largely unexplored, and this book presents a framework that emphasizes the factors that are relevant to and unique to the adoption of OSS. This framework was applied to five real-life case studies. Each case represents a story of adoption and outlines the practices and recommendations.

The aim is to clarify whether the adoption of OSS differs from the adoption of software that is not open source. The book analyzed the similarities and differences between the five cases and asked what is distinctive about these cases, all of which relate to OSS adoption.

The following cases were analyzed:

• The Irish Hibernia Hospital was an example of the success and failure of different OSS solutions.

• The Italian council, Südtiroler Gemeindenverband, was an example of the evolution of the adoption and assimilation stages with a specific focus on the bilingual customization of standards for services and documents.

• Extremadura in Spain was the case in which the entire region adopted a unique platform that was modeled for non-English speakers and their cultural traditions.

• The state of Massachusetts in the United States in which adoption primarily refers to the migration of data standards (e.g., document formats) as a means of increasing e-accessibility.

• The case of the Italian Chamber of Deputies had a high degree of lock-in with legacy systems, which determined a particular migration path that required migration of office systems before the migration of the operating system.

The following sections compare and contrast the five cases, identify the main ideas that emerged from the studies, show what is distinctive about OSS adoption by public organizations, and present some lessons and implications for practice.

MANAGERIAL INTERVENTION

The SGV case neatly explains the main issues faced by public sector organizations that lead them to consider OSS alternatives. These include a desire for lower costs, a lesser degree of vendor lock-in, more control over the development of the software, and the encouragement of the local software industry.

Mandatory versus Voluntary Usage

Open source projects in general, including these five cases studies, showed that there is often a clear need for strong leadership (von Hippel and von Krogh 2003). The Hibernia hospital case indicates that user participation and involvement in the decision-making process is necessary for the improvement of voluntary usage, but it is usually the case that strong leadership encourages user involvement. In other cases, such as SGV's and Massachusetts' policy for open standards, strong leadership became more relevant for the sustained, long-term use of OSS. Indeed, the Massachusetts study emphasizes how government management leadership experienced high points and low points on the road to the successful adoption of open document formats.

The level of software adoption within each of the five organizations was not uniform. The five organizations differed in their degree of adoption. Some cases, such as the Hibernia hospital, highlight how mandating software usage created different classes of users, which was largely a function of organizational hierarchy and only accentuated the existing hierarchical structure. For instance, those who were forced to adopt OSS felt that their skills and abilities were not appreciated.

Where the cases differed often concerned the degree and type of strategy used by management to create a positive atmosphere for OSS adoption. The motivation for OSS adoption differed across cases, which impacted adoption rates. When the Italian Chamber of Deputies moved to open source, it was driven by a need to cut costs, and any possible reduction in technical skills was not an issue. Management instead accentuated the similarities between the OSS product and the proprietary format that had been used previously. The Extremadura case showed how stakeholders contextualized the software into the local language and were innovative in their adaptation of the software, which represented a novel way of encouraging OSS adoption. There was also an emphasis on training and different training regimes in the Extremadura case. The major success factor was the establishment of a regional publicly funded software firm that partially developed the initial platform and then maintained that platform with new versions and upgrades. The software firm also provided documentation and ad hoc support for the deployment. The key success factor was that the decision was political and was implemented in the context of a holistic strategy for the entire region. This was possible because Extremadura initially had no IT infrastructure and no money with which to purchase an infrastructure.

Training and Support
As mentioned above, the Extremadura study highlights the value of training for easing adoption problems within an

organization. This feature is a key element of the SGV case, which shows how training was tailored to user needs and became a part of a toolbox for promoting adoption throughout the entire life cycle of the software. Training for the SGV management was obviously part of the long-term strategy for ensuring adoption and continued meaningful use. In cases in which the training was perfunctory and not tailored to user needs or part of a plan for sustained adoption, there was obvious resistance from users, as is evident in the Hibernia hospital case.

The manner of approaching training and its implementation in each case varied slightly, and the Italian Chamber of Deputies case was the most distinctive. The aim was to create an e-learning community in which employees would feel that they were improving their skills and that OSS was adding value. SGV management decided to hire external consultants, a move that had a positive effect on OSS adoption. Total cost of ownership (TCO) is a factor that is often insufficiently analyzed at the level of detail that is required to make a clear judgment concerning the supposed lower costs of OSS. The Hibernia hospital case focused to some degree on TCO, and one interesting point that emerged was the inclusion of training costs in TCO calculations. Organizations are likely to focus on the low licensing costs that OSS make possible, while ignoring other factors, such as training and software services and, most important of all, exit costs and legacy costs, which might result in expenditures being equivalent to, or even exceeding, those for proprietary software adoption. Russo and Succi (2009) proposed a model of TCO for migrations to OSS in public administrations. This study identified the significance of training costs during a migration to OSS.

Championing OSS Adoption

All of the studies found that championing initiatives was relevant. However, in some cases, such as the case of the Italian Chamber of Deputies, local champions who used OSS at home or work were involved in helping train others and in generating enthusiasm. This had the effect of bringing in genuine champions who used OSS by choice instead of by requirement. OSS development and contribution (patches or feedback) requires a certain level of expertise, so champions were respected members of the organization who had reputations for being highly skilled and knowledgeable. In the case of SGV, the CIO took on the role of champion and promoted OSS adoption both within the organization and externally in order to increase awareness of the initiative.

However, only the Extremadura case referred to championing in detail. This was a successful case, and one reason for its success was its promotion as an export flagship project for the rest of the country and for other parts of Europe.

SUBJECTIVE NORMS

Cultural issues of acceptance were linked to managerial intervention because the latter had a clear effect on the usage policies that were adopted by the organizations. In the cases in which OSS was mandatory for employees (e.g., Hibernia hospital, the Italian Chamber of Deputies, and SGV), there was a negative attitude toward OSS adoption. In the cases in which the management sought to counteract resistance through provision of tailored training, championing initiatives, and re-skilling efforts, adoption rates tended to be higher and sustainable over time.

One distinctive aspect was evident in the Massachusetts policy study, which demonstrated that pragmatism was more important than ideology (the latter is often associated with OSS adoption). Decisions on open formats and standards were based on considerations regarding what would be most effective rather than for the sake of openness. The same cannot be claimed for any of the other cases, which reveals a degree of pragmatism in Massachusetts' decision to adopt OSS. Managerial decisions were for the most part grounded in ideological or financial concerns.

FACILITATING CONDITIONS

Innovation Attributes

Relative Advantage
In four out of the five cases, there was a clear relative advantage when OSS was used. The strength of advantage varied, however. In the SGV case, the value was clear and evident. The ability and choice to adapt software, and make it backwardly compatible with older versions of proprietary software, made OSS use innovative and superior to proprietary products. The Massachusetts policy case demonstrated that open standard adoption by the government could reduce vendor lock-ins, and living documents could be produced that could be amended and improved, provided that multiple software implementations were interoperable and compatible with the open standard.

The Hibernia hospital case is the only one in which there was little evidence of relative advantage due to adoption. StarOffice produced negative perceptions of its image and functionality, which caused its usage to be seen as disadvantageous. The email platform, on the other hand, was regarded as being more of a back-office platform-type application and was perceived less negatively.

The belief that greater transparency in OSS can address security-related concerns was apparent in the Italian Chamber of Deputies case. The idea of security through openness was unique to this case, and none of the other organizations appeared to consider the idea of enhanced security through OSS as being relevant to their concerns.

Image

The manner in which OSS was viewed by users had a strong influence on short-term and long-term adoption, which suggests that image was an important factor. The technology offered something new and innovative, if only the idea that it was a pioneering project, as was the case for Extremadura. The image that was promoted internally and portrayed to the outside world was a key factor in the success of Extremadura. Three out of the five cases were pioneers in their fields and their countries.

The Hibernia hospital case tells another story—one of OSS being linked to the idea of de-skilling and unlearning marketable skills. The employees feared that they would have to learn skills that would set them back in their current jobs and make them less marketable in the future. This is quite different than the Italian Chamber of Deputies case, in which OSS was seen as a way to *re-skill* in office IT. The image of the innovation was thus the primary vulnerability in the Hibernia study. The degree of relevance of the image of a particular technology needs to be understood in the context of the organization, culture, and several other factors. The Hibernia case is unique because it provides us with insight into how the poor image of OSS that was linked to an open source product (one that was actually being used effectively by others around the world) played on the insecurities of the employees concerning their employment and promotion prospects.

In the Extremadura case, the government was able to leverage the idea that this was groundbreaking work that would serve as an example for the rest of the country. The high status attached to OSS in the Extremadura study was not apparent in the other cases. OSS was seen as an innovation that would lead to process innovation, which could then be transferred to other regions. The Massachusetts policy initiative was similar in its desire to lay the foundation for future use of OSS, document formats, and technology standards. However, while OSS relies on open standards, the reverse relationship is not as direct or necessary.

Observability

In three out of the five cases, observable innovation was considered important, either because it was lacking or because it helped create a better image for OSS. The more interesting case regarding a positive effect of observability is Extremadura, where being able to read and access the code was linked to how communication patterns, code changes, and availability of documentation helped provide clear evidence of the innovative qualities of OSS. The Hibernia hospital case contrasts with that of Extremadura. In the Extremadura case, the greater the observability, the better the attitude regarding the adoption of OSS. In the Hibernia hospital case, StarOffice was perceived as a failure, and the differences between StarOffice and Microsoft Office were purposefully minimized. Subsequent projects related to OSS were implemented without any highlighting of their open source nature.

In the Massachusetts policy case study, the issue of observability emerged not out of the fear of de-skilling but rather because OSS was observably less accessible and did not provide software support to the disabled. Although OSS was being used, development help was not sought or offered as a means of resolving this issue, and Microsoft products were considered to be more accessible for different types of users.

The Italian Chamber of Deputies case shows that adoption can be increased or at least resistance can be reduced, when it is not explicitly evident that the software being adopted is open source. The ability to open an ODF document that is sent as an attachment in an email and automatically converted into a Microsoft document promoted the adoption of OpenOffice. The compatibility issues were solved, and the software's open source nature became less observable.

Organizational Attributes

Absorptive Capacity

The cases indicate that achieving acceptance and sustained adoption required that OSS be understood in the context of the software products with which the employees were already familiar (von Hippel and von Krogh 2003). Learning how to use the new tool became easier and thus more acceptable. However, a balance must be struck between the extent to which OSS is seen as an improvement over the incumbent technology while also not appearing to be so innovative that it appears to involve too much change for new adopters. In order to handle this, management must understand the skill sets and needs of employees. A structured and tailored manner of training can be used to develop this balance, which is obvious in the success of the Extremadura case. The audience and users of the system were different than in the Hibernia hospital case; their approach involved focusing on the core internal developer group. The core group was encouraged to be a part of the software customization team, and this resulted in deep learning that improved the organization's ability to adopt OSS. Some organizations use a mix of training supplemented with the strategy of approaching a core group to appropriate the software as their own in order to improve absorptive capacity, as happened in the case of the Italian Chamber of Deputies.

Training and learning could thus be used to improve absorptive capacity, but only one case became a training translation that could be used by other regions and organizations. Extremadura was able to export its model of adoption and use. It changed its role from internal absorption to creating a model of OSS adoption that could be transferred to other Spanish-speaking regions and organizations. It was marketed as a flagship project in which participation was a privilege. The open format and standards idea of the Massachusetts policy study indicates that it sought to lay the foundation for a system that could be used by other states in the United States and other countries.

Another feature of the Extremadura case that helped to promote absorptive capacity was the development of OSS in the local language. This was possible because the code was open and accessible. This had other positive features, such as helping develop the local software industry to the extent of creating a digital ecosystem that was interdependent and sustainable.

The Massachusetts policy case was distinctive in relation to absorptive capacity because it approached creating open standards as a standard method of assessing TCO. In this particular study, TCO was something that needed to be investigated so that it could become transferable and give rise to increased OSS use. The aim was to create criteria for TCO measurement and analysis that other organizations could use at a later date. This is important, because TCO for OSS is difficult to assess because proprietary software may be more expensive at the outset but may also involve lower costs with respect to continued software support services in comparison with OSS.

DISTINCTIVE ISSUES WITH OSS ADOPTION

This chapter conducts a comparison of issues and how each organization attempted to resolve concerns about OSS adoption. There is a question regarding the extent to which the issues that arose for each organization stemmed from open source and would not have arisen with the adoption of proprietary software. The following section addresses this question.

Greater Adaptability of Software

The more successful cases of OSS adoption leveraged the ability to adapt code to local needs. This was feasible only because the source code was available and accessible, and the license allowed modifications to be made. Allowing users to play with the software, change it, and make it more native to the degrees that were achieved in the cases of the Italian Chamber of Deputies and Extremadura was possible only with OSS.

Need for Documentation and Promise of Support

There is often no guaranteed assurance of support for OSS, so this can be one reason why organizations would steer clear of it. OSS developers have a reputation—one that may be deserved—for poor documentation of code, a state of affairs which does not encourage companies or organizations to adopt it readily. There is a need for assurance and support in open source in comparison with proprietary software adoption (where it is usually part of the service level agreement).

Total Cost of Ownership

TCO for open source is often higher in the short run, due in part to training costs, costs related to software services, and legacy costs. The reduced costs that OSS can offer an organization are usually only possible in the long run (Stoller 2004). In the short run, the costs of training, adoption of new systems, and hiring of an in-house team or third party to maintain the software are not very different for OSS and proprietary software. However, in the long run, lower licensing costs become increasingly significant, and the adopting organization can find OSS adoption to be efficient and productive. Another interesting part of TCO is exit costs. This is true for the adoption of proprietary products as well as for OSS. Companies feel secure when they hold the source code, which means that changing vendors or support will be straightforward. However, experience with OSS adoption has shown that exit costs are related to the lack of access to the tacit knowledge of the original developers, and this can be exacerbated by the fact that code documentation may be incomplete.

Studies have shown that legacy costs in many areas, including mainframes, are higher in comparison with open source alternatives. Shanker (2008) points out that mainframe vendors, when engaged in defensive preparation for the emergence of open source alternatives, developed appropriate partitioning strategies to stave off their demise. However, Shanker shows how there were two cases in which there was a 305% return on investment over a four-year period when an open source system was used. So, although mainframes held their own for a short period of time, open source cost savings and higher return on investment eventually made mainframes less relevant.

High-Profile Developers

In the OSS community, there are examples of high-profile developers who have contributed code or become a part of a project, which increased their chances of survival. Champions are necessary in OSS. Open source projects are often rooted in a reputation-based meritocracy, and a high-profile developer with respected skills can be a persuasive champion. Proprietary projects need champions, but this feature is also important for OSS adoption.

Practical Decision-Making

OSS developers are often characterized as being ideologically motivated (Stewart and Gosain 2006). However, studies have shown that OSS developers, like other types of developers, are guided by practical decision-making (Wayner 2000). Their aim is to use anything that will fix the problem. Ideology may well be discussed, but pragmatic decisions are in the forefront in most OSS projects.

Enhanced Security

The case studies in this book, particularly the SGV case, show how OSS made innovation possible and visible. Greater visibility and accessibility to the source is possible with OSS licenses and can help create more secure systems (Fitzgerald and Feller 2002; Hoepman and Jacobs 2007). The theory behind this claim is that visibility makes it possible for many parties to become aware of the problem, which increases the pool of talent with the ability to fix the problem. A number of studies have shown that there is greater security when OSS is used, but some commercial and public organizations continue to be reluctant to adopt software that might turn out to be breakable due to high access levels. However, a counterargument has been advanced that suggests that hesitance to adopt OSS has less to do with security issues and more to do with perceived intellectual-property-rights (IPR) concerns.

Access through Openness

Openness of code, licenses, and communication channels and access to archival material and developer contributions—these are aspects that are only possible with OSS. Thus, the development process for OSS is also more visible. In principle, this offers the possibility of reducing vendor lock-ins if there are multiple interoperable software implementations. Again, this may not be possible with many types of proprietary software.

CONCLUSIONS: LESSONS AND RECOMMENDATIONS

This book examines OSS adoption in public organizations. The five case studies provide a glimpse of the paths taken by organizations that adopted OSS. The book draws on the framework in chapter 2 to analyze these cases and develop an understanding of the problems faced by organizations and the strategies they adopted to address these issues. This section includes lessons for practitioners and other organizations that may be considering the adoption of OSS. As is the case with other types of change, moving to OSS can be difficult. While the benefits can be great, the migration can also encounter resistance, be destructive to morale, or turn out to be a complete failure. A summary of the comparison of the five case studies is provided in table 8.1.

Training
It is apparent that there is a need for public organizations to take training for OSS adoption seriously. There must be a clear plan for training, and it must not end with a limited amount of short-term training during the early stage of implementation. A phased, highly contextualized (with respect to the organization's needs), and made-to-measure training plan for different job roles should be required. Long-term enthusiasm and sustained adoption is possible with systematic, planned training over the life cycle of software use within an organization. The aim of the training is to improve the relationship between the user and the software by creating awareness and positive rapport. Increased user awareness can promote the positive adoption of technology.

Comprehensive and Nonexclusive Approach to Adoption
The cases reveal how mandating usage for some categories of users has created problems. Usage should not be a function of one's position in the organization hierarchy, because this accentuates differences. Permission to opt out of usage should not be seen as a privilege for the "more important" employees. Organizations should instead practice the blanket implementation and adoption of any form of OSS (as in the case

Table 8.1
Comparison of Five Case Studies

	Overlap in cases	Difference in cases	Distinctive of OSS	Lessons for practice
Managerial intervention				
Mandatory vs. voluntary usage	Strong leadership was needed, and there was creation of different classes of users who are mapped to the hierarchy of the organization.	Awareness was created in different ways in each case. Motivation for adoption also varied in each case.		Open source infrastructural software will be easier to implement than application software with varied users. A clear plan for training and creating awareness is needed.
Training and support	Resistance was a bigger problem where training was not customized.	The Italian Chamber case indicates that an e-learning community was set up to ensure interest and use. SGV hired external consultants. TCO in relation to training was mentioned only in the Irish Hibernia Hospital case.	TCO is higher for OSS in the short term due to training costs. OSS cost benefits are possible in long run.	Comprehensive and tailored training is needed for successful adoption of OSS.

Table 8.1
(continued)

	Overlap in cases	Difference in cases	Distinctive of OSS	Lessons for practice
Championing OSS	The Italian Chamber case used local champions familiar with OSS to train and create enthusiasm.	The Extremadura case used championing schemes to make OSS adoption successful and a flagship project.	High-profile developer contributions increase chances of survival, so champions are needed in OSS.	Champions are needed for adoption, so this element should be built into specific job roles in organizations.
Subjective norms				
	Managerial intervention using force had a negative effect on OSS adoption.	Pragmatism was given precedence over OSS ideology in the Massachusetts policy case study.	OSS developer decisions are often predicated on pragmatism rather than ideology.	—
Facilitating conditions: Innovation attributes				
Relative advantage	SGV case adapted OSS software for backward compatibility, even with proprietary software. The Massachusetts policy case promoted open standards adoption to reduce vendor lock-in.	The Irish Hibernia Hospital case showed little advantage with OSS adoption. Workers using it were seen as less-skilled employees. Security linked to greater transparency in OSS was made apparent in the Italian Chamber case.	The SGV case shows how OSS made innovation possible and visible! Greater visibility possible with the openness of OSS can create more secure systems.	Open standards and formats provide public organizations with a way to create more secure and transparent systems.

Table 8.1
(continued)

	Overlap in cases	Difference in cases	Distinctive of OSS	Lessons for practice
Image	The Irish Hibernia Hospital case shows OSS being linked to de-skilling and unlearning of marketable skills for users. But in the Italian Chamber case, OSS was seen as a way to re-skill in office IT.	Extremadura case was able to leverage the idea of OSS adoption as a flagship project to be copied by others. OSS was seen as an innovation that would lead to process innovations that could be transferred to other regions.	—	Follow examples of successful OSS adoption by private companies. They align themselves to developers and open source projects to create innovations.
Observability	Innovation was a key reason for OSS adoption in all of the cases.	The Extremadura case showed how observability of code was linked to code changes and documentation availability. The Massachusetts policy case was less accessible for the physically challenged users. The ability to open an ODF document in the Italian Chamber case as a Microsoft document allowed greater adoption of OpenOffice.	Openness of code and licenses, archival material, and developer contributions are only really possible with OSS.	—

Table 8.1
(continued)

Facilitating conditions: Organizational attributes

	Overlap in cases	Difference in cases	Distinctive of OSS	Lessons for practice
Absorptive capacity	Learning a new tool is easier when the formats are similar, and users are comfortable.	Training and learning were methods used to improve absorptive capacity. Only the Extremadura case became a "training transla-tion" for other regions and organizations. The Extremadura case adapted OSS to local language for greater acceptance. The Massachusetts policy case discussed modeling TCO to make it transferable to other states and organizations.	Allowing users to change software and make it "native" is only possible with OSS as seen in the Italian Chamber and Ex-tremadura cases.	Software will be adopted more readily if users feel they are part of its creation and implementation. This could be seen as part of training or software cocreation.

of the adoption of Symphony (OpenOffice) by IBM (Linux Magazine 2009)).

Maintenance and Support

OSS, even more so than proprietary software, should come with a guarantee of support and maintenance. The source code is available, but having it available does not signify that maintenance will necessarily be easy. Indeed, the tacit knowledge involved in initially creating that software cannot be derived simply by accessing the source code. The rationale behind software design decisions, which can be crucially important, remains opaque. Thus, access to the development community and/or detailed documentation is necessary. Maintaining an in-house core team of developers to work alongside external vendors and support companies can help to ensure that a degree of tacit knowledge will always remain within the organization. In addition, many of the benefits of OSS cannot be realized without truly interoperable software implementations. Interoperability among software implementations requires continued software maintenance, testing, and support.

Access to Open Source Communities

Private companies align themselves with successful developers and open source project communities in order to create more innovative software and develop and maintain a positive internal and external image with members of the development community. Public sector organizations should consider this option, because the number of knowledgeable developers with ideas for improvement and innovation continues to increase. The process of reaching out to open source communities requires the commitment of resources, a factor which has shown to be useful in studies on OSS adoption conducted by private companies (e.g., Agerfalk and Fitzgerald 2008).

Security through Openness

Open source and open standards can provide public organizations with a way to create more secure and transparent systems that can be used for purposes of interacting with employees and with customers (the general public). In many situations, openness can help create more secure systems, and the possibility of fixing lapses is greater when the actual source code is available for scrutiny and modification.

Adoption through Cocreation

Software, whether open source or proprietary, will be adopted more readily if users feel that they play a role in its creation and implementation. Given the openness of its licensing and development process, OSS makes cocreation attractive and almost inevitable (Prahalad and Ramaswamy 2002, 2004). Cocreation is one method of improving the chances of sustained adoption of software that can help reduce the costs of training and reduce user resistance.

Notes

Chapter 2

1. <http://ec.europa.eu/idabc>, etc.

Chapter 3

1. The name has been changed to preserve anonymity.

Chapter 4

1. COSPA, a consortium for OSS in public administrations (<http://www.cospa-project.org>), is an FP6 project funded through the European Commission (IST-STREP European project Nr. 002164, 2004–2006).

2. The FUSS project (<http://www.fuss.bz.it>) was funded by the Italian Scholastic Intendancy of the Province of Bolzano-Bozen and the European Social Fund.

3. Base is the component of the OpenOffice suite that manipulates database data. It enables users to create and modify tables, forms, queries, and reports, using either their own databases or Base's built-in database engine.

4. Calc is the spreadsheet component of OpenOffice.

5. The manual was the first user guide for OpenOffice (the team of OpenOffice at the time did not supply one) and helped the numerous other interested users who contacted the COSPA experts.

6. VNC is a platform-independent remote desktop protocol for remotely controlling another computer.

7. PROM (<http://www.prom.case.unibz.it>) and FLEA (<http://www.cospa-project.org/Assets/documents/Deliverables/D2.2 -CatalogueOfODSusedInPA.pdf>) were used to record which files were accessed and how many events each file experienced.

Chapter 6

1. The authors are grateful to the contributions of Dr. Rajiv Shah to this chapter.

Chapter 7

1. The authors are grateful to the contributions of Dr. Francesco di Cerbo to this chapter.

2. <http://www.moodle.org>.

References

Agerfalk, P., and B. Fitzgerald. 2008. Outsourcing to an unknown workforce: Exploring opensourcing as a global sourcing strategy. *Management Information Systems Quarterly* 32 (2): 385–410.

Asay, Matt. 2006. Open source and the commodity urge: Disruptive models for a disruptive development process. In *Open Sources 2.0: The Continuing Evolution*, ed. Chris DiBona, Danese Cooper, and Mark Stone. Sebastopol, CA: O'Reilly.

Ajzen, I. 1985. From intentions to actions: A theory of planned behaviour. In *Action control: From cognition to behaviour*, edited by J. Kuhl and J. Beckmann, 11–39. New York: Springer-Verlag.

Bajaj, A. 2000. A Study of Senior Information Systems Manager's Decision Models in Adopting New Computing Architectures. *Journal of the Association for Information Systems* 1 (4):1–56.

Bowman, L. 2003. Open-source battle rages in Oregon. CNET News. <http://news.cnet.com/2100-1012-996210.html>.

Bradford, M., and J. Florin. 2003. Examining the role of innovation diffusion factors on the implementation success of enterprise resource planning systems. *Information Systems* 4:205–225.

Burton-Jones, A., and M. J. Gallivan. 2007. Toward a deeper understanding of system usage in organizations: A multilevel perspective. *Management Information Systems Quarterly* 31 (4): 657–679.

Chau, P., and K. Tam. 1997. Factors affecting the adoption of open systems: An exploratory study. *Management Information Systems Quarterly* 21 (1): 1–24.

Chief Information Officer Council, UK Government. 2007. Transformational government enabled by technology. Accessed May 2010. <http://kbeg.case.unibz.it:8080/Plone/References/Transformational GovernmentEnabledByTechnology.pdf/view>.

Cohen, W. M., and D. A. Levinthal. 1990. Absorptive capacity: A new perspective on learning and innovation. *Administrative Science Quarterly* 35 (1): 128–152.

Committee for Economic Development. 2006. Open standards, open source, and open innovation: Harnessing the benefits of openness. Washington, D.C. Accessed August 2010. <http://www.ced.org/images/library/reports/digital_economy/report_ecom_open standards.pdf>.

Commonwealth of Massachusetts. 2008. Enterprise technical reference model—service oriented architecture (ETRM v. 5.0). Accessed January 2009. <http://www.mass.gov>.

Commonwealth of Massachusetts ITD. 2004a. Enterprise information technology acquisition policy (No. ITD-APP-02). Accessed January 2009. <http://www.mass.gov/Aitd/docs/policies_standards/itacquisitionpolicy.pdf>.

———. 2004b. Enterprise open standards policy (No. ITD-APP-01). Accessed January 2009. <http://www.mass.gov/Aitd/docs/policies _standards/openstandards.pdf>.

Compeau, D. R., and C. A. Higgins. 1995. Application of social cognitive theory to training for computer skills. *Information Systems Research* 6 (2): 118–143.

Cooper, R. B., and R. W. Zmud. 1990. Information technology implementation research: A technological diffusion approach. *Management Science* 36 (2): 123–139.

Davis, F. 1989. Perceived usefulness, perceived ease of use, and user acceptance of information technology. *Management Information Systems Quarterly* 13:319–340.

Di Bona, C., S. Ockman, and M. Stone, eds. 1999. *Open sources: Voices from the open source revolution.* Sebastopol, CA: O'Reilly.

Eveland, J., and L. Tornatzky. 1990. The deployment of technology. In *The Processes of Technological Innovation*, ed. L. Tornatzky and M. Fleischer. Lexington, MA: Lexington Books.

Eures. 2010. Labor Market Information, Extremadura, Spain. Accessed January 2011. <http://ec.europa.eu/eures/main.jsp?acro=lw &lang=en&catId=490&parentId=0>.

Feller, J., and B. Fitzgerald. 2002. *Understanding open source software development*. London: Addison-Wesley.

———. 1992. Information technology diffusion: A review of empirical research. In *Proceedings of the 13th International Conference on Information Systems*, edited by J. I. DeGross, J. D. Becker, and J. J. Elam, Dallas, TX, 195–206.

Fichman, R. G., and C. F. Kemerer. 1999. The illusory diffusion of innovation: An examination of assimilation gaps. *Information Systems Research* 10 (3): 255–275.

———. 1997. The assimilation of software process innovations: An organizational learning perspective. *Management Science* 43 (10): 1345–1363.

Fishbein, M., and I. Ajzen. 1975. *Belief, attitude, intention, and behaviour: An introduction to theory and research*. Reading, MA: Addison-Wesley.

Fitzgerald, B. 2009. Open source software implementation: Anatomy of success and failure. *International Journal of Open Source Software and Processes* 1 (1): 1–19.

———. 2006. The transformation of open source software. *Management Information Systems Quarterly* 30 (3): 587–598.

Fitzgerald, B., and J. Feller. 2002. A further investigation of open source software: Community, co-ordination, code quality and security issues. *Information Systems Journal* 12 (1): 3–6.

Fitzgerald, B., and T. Kenny. 2003. Open source software in the trenches: Lessons from a large scale implementation. In *Proceedings of 24 International Conference on Information Systems*, edited by T. March, A. Massey, and J. I. DeGross, Seattle, WA, December 14–17, 2003, 316–326.

Fuggetta, A. 2003. Open source software—an evaluation. *Journal of Systems and Software* 66 (1): 77–90.

FUNDECYT. 2008. Strategy in the information society. Accessed August 2010. <http://unpan1.un.org/intradoc/groups/public/documents/gaid/unpan033118.pdf>.

Gallego, M. D., P. Luna, and S. Bueno. 2008. User acceptance model of open source software. *Computers in Human Behavior* 24: 2199–2216.

Gallivan, M. 2001. Organizational adoption and assimilation of complex technological innovations: Development and application of a new framework. *Database* 32 (3): 51–85.

Gardner, W. D. 2005. OpenDocument policy challenged by disabled. *Information Week*.

Glynn, G., B. Fitzgerald, and C. Exton. 2005. Commercial adoption of open source software: An empirical study. In *Proceedings of International Symposium on Empirical Software Engineering*, Noosa Heads, Australia, November 17–18, 2005, 225–234.

Hoepman, J.-H., and B. Jacobs. 2007. Increased security through open source. *Communications of the ACM* 50 (1): 79–83.

IDABC. 2007. IDABC OSS Event 2007 in Badajoz. Accessed December 2010. <http://ec.europa.eu/idabc/en/chapter/5932.html>.

Krechmer, K. 2006. The meaning of open standards. *International Journal of IT Standards and Standardization Research* 4 (1): 43–61.

Kuk, G. 2006. Strategic interaction and knowledge sharing in the KDE developer mailing list. *Management Science* 52 (7): 1031–1042.

Kwon, T. H., and R. W. Zmud. 1987. Unifying the Fragmented Models of Information Systems Implementations. In *Critical Issues in Information Systems Research*, ed. R. Boland and R. Hirschheim, 227–252. Chichester, UK: John Wiley & Sons, Ltd.

Lai, E. 2007a. In about-face, Mass. now likely to OK Microsoft's OOXML; Latest state IT proposal lists Office format as acceptable open standard. *Computerworld 3*. Accessed December 2010. <http://www.computerworld.com/s/article/9026082/In_about_face_Mass._now_likely_to_OK_Microsoft_s_OOXML?intsrc=hm_list>.

———. 2007b. State's move to open document formats still not a mass migration. *Computerworld* 41 (24): 14.

Lakhani, K., and B. Wolf. 2005. Why hackers do what they do: Understanding motivation and effort in free/open source software projects. In *Perspectives on free and open source software*, edited by J. Feller, B. Fitzgerald, S. Hissam, and K. Lakhani, 3–22. Cambridge, MA: MIT Press.

Linux Magazine. 2009. IBM throws out Microsoft Office, Linux Magazine. Accessed August 2010. <http://www.linux-magazine.com/Online/News/IBM-Throws-Out-Microsoft-Office>.

Marks, R. B. 2004. Government/industry interactions in the global standards system. In *The standards edge: Dynamic tension*, edited by S. Bolin, 103–114. Ann Arbor, MI: Bolin Communication.

Markus, M. L. 1987. Toward a "critical mass" theory of interactive media: Universal access, interdependence and diffusion. *Communication Research* 14:491–511.

Massachusetts Information Technology Commission. 2003. Commonwealth of Massachusetts enterprise IT strategy. Accessed March 2010. <http://www.mass.gov>.

McCue, A. 2004. London council ditches Linux plans. Accessed January 2007. <http://news.zdnet.co.uk/software/0,1000000121,3911 8909,00.htm>.

Moore, G. C., and I. Benbasat. 1991. Development of an instrument to measure perceptions of adapting an information technology innovation. *Information Systems Research* 2 (3): 192–222.

Myers, S., and D. G. Marquis. 1969. *Successful industrial innovation: A study of factors underlying innovation in selected firms*, 69–71. National Science Foundation.

New York State Chief Information Officer. 2008. A strategy for openness: Enhancing e-records access in New York state. Accessed January 2009. <http://www.oft.state.ny.us/Policy/ESRA/erecords/PartIerecordsStudy.pdf>.

Niccolai, J. 2005. Scottish police pick Windows in software line-up. *InfoWorld*. Accessed December 2006. <http://www.infoworld.com/article/05/08/11/HNscottishpolice_1.html>.

Noyes, J. 2006. Technology today; ODF angers disabled workers. *Boston Herald*, 27.

Office of Government Commerce. 2004. Open source software: Use within UK government. Accessed January 2009. <http://www.govtalk.gov.uk/documents/oss_policy_version2.pdf>.

Office of the State Auditor. 2006. The examination of the information technology division's policy for implementing the open document standard. Boston, MA. Accessed January 2009. <http://www.mass.gov/sao/Audit%20Reports/2008/200608844t.pdf>.

Orlikowski, W. 1993. CASE tools are organizational change: Investigating Incremental and Radical Changes in Systems Development. *Management Information Systems Quarterly* 17 (3): 309–340.

Ozel, B., U. Jovanovic, B. Oba, and M. van Leeuwen. 2007. Perceptions on F/OSS Adoption. In *Open Source Development, Adoption and Innovation IFIP Working Group 2.13 on Open Source Software*, Limerick, Ireland, June 11–14, 2007.

Pepoli, B., and H. Dormitzer. 2007. Statement on ETRM v4.0 public review comments—August 1, 2007. Accessed December 2008. <http://xml.coverpages.org/ITD-ETRMv40-Statement.html>.

Peterson, S. 2004. The open road. *Government Technology*. Accessed January 2009. <http://www.govtech.com/gt/articles/87471>.

Prahalad, C. K., and V. Ramaswamy. 2004. Co-creating unique value with customers. *Strategy and Leadership* 32 (3): 4–9.

———. 2002. The co-creation connection. *Strategy and Business* 27 (2): 50–61.

Quinn, P. 2006. The policy, planning and pragmatic reasons for the Massachusetts move into OpenDocument. Accessed October 2008. <http://www.slideshare.net/jza/the-policy-planning-and -pragmatic-reasons>.

Roberts, J., I.-H. Hann, and S. Slaughter. 2006. Understanding the Motivations, Participation, and Performance of Open Source Software Developers: a Longitudinal Study of the Apache Projects. *Management Science* 52 (7): 984–999.

Rogers, E. 1996. *Diffusion of innovations*. 4th ed. New York: Free Press.

Rogers, E. 2003. *Diffusion of innovations*. 5th ed. New York: Free Press.

———. 1962. *Diffusion of innovations*. New York: Free Press.

Rogers, E. M., and F. F. Shoemaker. 1972. *Communication of innovations: A cross-cultural approach*. 2nd ed. New York: Free Press.

Rossi, B., B. Russo, and G. Succi. 2007. Evaluation of a migration to open source software. In *Handbook of research on open source software: Technological, economic and social perspectives*, edited by K. St. Amant and B. Still, 400. IGI Global.

————. 2006a. A study on the introduction of open source software in the public administration. In *Proceedings of the conference Open Source Systems, IFIP Working Group 2.13 Foundation on Open Source Software*, Como, Italy, June 8–10, 2006, 165–171.

————. 2006b. COSPA (consortium for studying, evaluating, and supporting the introduction of open source software and open data standards in the public administration). In *Proceedings of the 2006 national conference on digital government research*, DG.O 2006, San Diego, CA, May 21–24, 2006, 153–154.

Russo, B., B. Braghin, P. Gasperi, A. Sillitti, and G. Succi. 2005. Defining TCO for the transition to open source systems. In *Proceedings of the First International Conference on Open Source*, OSS2005, Genoa, Italy, July 11–15, 2005, 108–112.

Russo, B., and G. Succi. 2009. A cost model of open source adoption. In *Handbook of research on ICT-enabled transformational government: A global perspective*, edited by V. Weerakkody, M. Janssen, and Y. K. Dwivedi, 582. Information Science Publishing.

Russo, B., G. Succi, and P. Zuliani. 2003. Toward an empirical assessment of the benefits of open source software. In *Proceedings of the 3rd Workshop on Open Source Software Engineering: Taking Stock of the Bazar,* collocated with ICSE'03, International Conference on Software Engineering, Portland, OR, May 3–10, 2003, 117–120.

Sanders, J. 1998. Linux, open source, and software's future. *IEEE Software* 15 (5): 88–91.

Senate Committee on Post Audit and Oversight, Commonwealth of Massachusetts. 2006. Open standards, closed government. Accessed January 2009. <http://www.mass.gov/legis/bills/senate/st02/st02612.htm>.

Shah, R. C., J. P. Kesan, and A. Kennis. 2008. Lessons for government adoption of open standards: A case study of the Massachusetts policy. *Journal of Information Technology & Politics* 5 (4): 387–398.

Shaikh, M. 2007. Version control software in the open source process: A performative view of learning and organizing in the Linux Collectif. Unpublished Thesis. London School of Economics.

Shanker, G. 2008. Mainframe migration case studies: A total cost of ownership comparison. Orlando, FL: Allinean Inc. Accessed August 2010. <http://www.alinean.com/PDFs/Intel-Mainframe_Migration -TCOStudy.pdf>.

Stallman, R. 2002. Free software reality v. perception: Letter to the editor. *Communications of the ACM* 45 (7): 11–12.

Stewart, K., and S. Gosain. 2006. The impact of ideology on effectiveness in open source software development teams. *Management Information Systems Quarterly* 30 (2): 291–314.

Stoller, J. 2004. Open source: Assessing the TCO picture. *CMA Management* 78 (5): 18–22.

Succi, G., and P. Zuliani. 2004. Exploiting the collaboration between open source and research. In *Proceedings of the 4th Workshop on Open Source Software Engineering*, ICSE 2004, Edinburgh, Scotland, May 23–28, 2004, 97–99.

Swanson, E. B. 1994. Information Systems Innovation among Organizations. *Management Science* 40 (9):1069–1092.

Taylor, S., and P. Todd. 1995. Understanding IT usage: A test of competing models. *Information Systems Research* 6 (2):144–176.

Thurston, R. 2006. Criticism mounts over Birmingham's Linux project. Accessed January 2007. <http://www.zdnet.com.au/news/ software/soa/Criticism_mounts_over_Birmingham_s_Linux_project/ 0,130061733,339272293,00.htm>.

Tornatzky, L., and K. Klein. 1982. Innovation characteristics and innovation adoption implementation: A meta-analysis of findings. *IEEE Transactions on Engineering Management* 29 (1): 28–45.

Trott, P. 1998. *Innovation management and new product development*. Harlow, UK: Pearson Education Limited.

Turner, A. 2005. Linux misses Windows of opportunity. Accessed January 2007. <http://www.theage.com.au/articles/2005/09/ 26/1127586780339.html?from=top5>.

Updegrove, A. 2008. Odf vs. Ooxml: War of the Words Chapter 5. Accessed August 2008. <http://www.consortiuminfo.org/standards blog/index.php?topic=20071125145019553>.

Vaas, L. 2003. Road to open source. *Eweek*.

van de Ven, A. H., D. E. Polley, R. Garud, and S. Venkataraman. 2008. *The Innovation Journey*. New York: Oxford University Press.

van Reijswoud, V. 2005. OSS for development: Myth or reality? Accessed January 2007. <http://www.calibre.ie/events/limerick/docs/calibre_Reijswoud_presentation.pdf>.

Ven, K., D. Van Nuffel, and J. Verelst. 2006. The introduction of OpenOffice.org on the Brussels public administration. In *Proceedings of the conference Open Source Systems, IFIP Working Group 2.13 Foundation on Open Source Software*, edited by E. Damiani, B. Fitzgerald, W. Scacchi, and G. Succi, Como, Italy, June 8–10, 2006, 123–134.

von Hippel, E., and G. von Krogh. 2003. Open source software and the "private-collective" innovation model: Issues for organization science. *Organization Science* 14 (2): 209–223.

Wayner, P. 2000. *Free for all: How Linux and the free software movement undercut the high-tech titans*. New York: HarperCollins.

Weber, M. 1948. *From Max Weber: Essays in sociology*, edited by H. H. Gerth and W. Mills. London: Routledge.

Weisman, R. 2005. Microsoft fights bid to drop office software. *Boston Globe*. Accessed March 2010. <http://www.boston.com/business/technology>.

West, J. 2007. The economic realities of open standards: Black, white and many shades of gray. In *Standards and public policy*, edited by S. Greenstein and V. Stango, 87–122. Cambridge: Cambridge University Press.

Zachary, G. 2003. Ghana, information technology and development in Africa. Accessed August 2006. <http://www.cspo.org/products/articles/BlackStar.PDF>.

Index